STRUCTURING
THE VOID

STRUCTURING

THE VOID

The Struggle for Subject in

Contemporary American Fiction

Jerome Klinkowitz

DUKE UNIVERSITY PRESS   DURHAM & LONDON 1992

For

Jonathan

and

Nina

Contents

Acknowledgments

Structuring the Void is both a retrospective and projective work, reaching back to an author I first studied over twenty years ago and looking forward to others, publishing just recently, who in my estimation carry forward traditions established by Kurt Vonnegut, Richard Brautigan, and others who first reached a wide public during the great outflowing of innovative fiction in the 1960s.

Throughout my own twenty years as a literary scholar and critic the sole source of support for my work has been the University of Northern Iowa. For this present book the university provided a sabbatical and much continuing help, not the least of it being to supply me with students willing to trust their undergraduate educations to texts written by the writers studied here. It is they who best confirm one's sense of an ongoing literary history. My own children are themselves college students now, at the University of Iowa and Loyola University, and it is a pleasure to see novels not yet published when they were born and writers they met as casual visitors to our home appearing on their own course booklists. The literature of *Structuring the Void* is uniquely their own.—Jerome Klinkowitz

1

Structuring

the

Void

"What do we talk about when we talk about love?" asks one of contemporary fiction's most revealing titles. Its dilemma in describing the immense amount of activity centering around something that can never be satisfactorily defined reflects a problem common to many other postmodern pursuits. What is it, for example, that theologians discuss, when their own theology says God no longer exists? And what do painters paint when the best of them claim that their canvases are not surfaces upon which to represent but rather arenas within which to act? Granted, their painting becomes its own subject, just as discussions of the death of God keep the concept alive. But if the subject matter itself has been declared nonexistent, one can hardly say that the acts of painting or discussing are of thematic or even topical pertinence, for the whole question of being "about" something has become invalid.

For fiction, made as it is of words, the problem is even more obvious. Words are signs, and signs by nature refer to something other than themselves; the four alphabetic characters that spell out "tree" have for their subject the deciduous or coniferous woody plant which additional words can then specify. Deconstructive philosophy teaches that we are never really talking about things, only the relationships between them—specifically those relations that indicate what the thing is not. Again, the basis is linguistic: the object spelled out by the three letters of "cat" is not necessarily the feline animal we picture in terms of following the sign to its object of reference, but rather something other than all the things the substitution of twenty-five other letters in each slot would indicate—"rat," "hat," "mat," and so forth ad infinitum.

And these are simply the linguistic and philosophic considerations. Taking fiction on its most traditional terms, the crisis is even more acute. For if a novel or short story is supposed to provide, in imaginatively creative form, news from the world, then what in fact can its subject be when the entire notion of being "about" something has become a circular question? Yet, just as theologians talk and painters paint, fiction writers continue to write, and their books are filled with ostensible content. There are even, in these postmodern times, love stories. But what in fact do we write about when we write about love?

The answer involves devising for fiction an understanding similar to the deconstructive philosophers' interpretation of knowledge as a comprehension of system rather than substance and abstract artists' appreciation of painting as expression rather than illustration. Writers surely create something, but their fiction is no longer seen best in terms of subject or even content, but rather as a structuring act that becomes its own reality. Thus even though all material claims yield only a void, it is a structured void, with the fiction writer's acts creating a systematic web of relationships that is sustained not by what it captures or spans but rather by its own network of constructions.

Structuring the void turns out to be what many of the innovative fiction writers of the American 1960s were up to. Their movement was the first in several generations—since the 1920s, in fact—to mount a programmatic challenge against established conventions, and at the time much of their exuberance was attributed to the customary rambunctiousness of revolution and the almost sexual thrill of overthrowing staid authority. Needless to say, there was much rowdiness and lack of inhibition in the air, and some of the period's novels—notably those following the line from Ken Kesey's *One Flew Over the Cuckoo's Nest* to Richard Fariña's *Been Down So Long It Looks Like Up to Me* and Tom Robbins's *Another Roadside Attraction*—rely more heavily on revolutionary themes than techniques and therefore, like the black humor fiction of the late fifties and earlier sixties by the likes of Terry Southern and Bruce Jay Friedman, spend a great deal of time calling for an aesthetic revolt while sustaining the literary forms used by those they claim to be the oppressors. Yet a quarter century's hindsight reveals that the highest stylistic profiles—the fiction of Richard Brautigan, Ishmael Reed, and Ronald Sukenick, for example—are achieved not by prescriptions for new social, political, and behavioral structures but by acts of nonreferential structurings themselves.

Consider the free-floating ideas in Richard Brautigan's works: "in watermelon sugar" and "trout fishing in America," which on their ways to becoming titles for novels are cast about like themes in search of references, concepts in search of philosophies, or principles in search of beliefs. Though each is repeated scores of times, neither is allowed to attach itself to or even become the expression of any truly referential material. The phrase can identify a character, a place, or an attitude, its very interchangeability of reference eclipsing the notion of reference itself. Along the way Brautigan does so much else with language—notably lengthening the gap in metaphors between tenor and vehicle so that all sense of comparison is forgotten in the simple joy of having bridged such distance—that the resultant narrative becomes nothing more than a delightful exercise in imaginative flexibility and expansion. From *Trout Fishing in America* (San Francisco: Four Seasons Foundation, 1967) one recalls not the central character (for there is none) or the novel's theme (which is so general as to be a celebration of the imagination itself) but rather the comparisons, both expressed and implied, such as a neglected graveyard for paupers whose grass has "turned a flat-tire brown in the summer and stayed that way until the rain, like a mechanic, began in the late autumn" and then the rain itself doing its work "like a sleepy short-order cook cracking eggs over a grill next to a railroad station" (pp. 20–21). The distance between "grass" and "flat tire" is immense, and the act of joining the two to prompt the reader's insight is truly inspired, but what makes a narrative happen within the language itself is the orderly sequential and developmental movement between "flat-tire" and "mechanic," which yields a world in action. Yet for all temptations to make reference to an outward reality, the initial improbability of joining tenor and vehicle make the sentence an experience of aesthetics rather than of the world.

A decade and a half later, near the end of his life in the culturally different (and certainly alien) 1980s, Brautigan's most characteristic style still avoided reporting about the world in favor of structuring the void. In his last novel, *So the Wind Won't Blow It All Away* (New York: Delacorte Press/Seymour Lawrence, 1982), he transposes his approach to language to the notion of time, which is also seen more as a system of differences than for anything of substance in itself. When Brautigan's narrator puts himself back into the past for the occasion of writing this book, he finds himself dealing with several layers of narrative existence, from the present in which he works (the 1980s) through the 1940s events narrated to the various objects of an even more distant past the narrator-as-a-boy discovered back then, such as an ancient perambulator: "I walked very carefully over to the baby buggy. I didn't want to stumble over the past and break my present-tense leg that might leave me crippled in the future. I took the handle of the baby buggy and pulled it away from the 1900s and into the year 1947" (p. 11). What the narrator does here is give the reader a sense of "one's time and life on earth" not by concocting a referential theme but rather demonstrating its effect in a structural composition, suspending 1900, 1947, and 1982 in a continuum supported only by his storytelling presence and the reader's act as audience to it. Sometimes syntax alone can do it, as when following an uneventful morning one can note that "The sun had reversed its boredom and now had grown interesting as it began its descent which would soon open the beginning doors of night and the wind had died down making the pond as still and quiet as sleeping glass" (pp. 55–56). The antihierarchal nature of the conjunction *and* clears the way for letting poetic fancy and natural observation blend into one seamless text of narrative, anchored only by the metaphoric junction of "sleeping" and "glass."

What Richard Brautigan does with time, Ishmael Reed does with history. In the hands of novelists and new journalists from Norman Mailer to Hunter S. Thompson, history had lost its problematic nature (think of all those devilings of Faulkner and Wolfe) and become something to be played with rather than played by, less a source of nightmare and inhibition than a field for exuberant action—in other words not as a determining subject but as a void within which one could pose endless structures. Reed's own belief in the comparative, pluralistic view of multiculturalism (not one history but many different histories, much like Bakhtin's polyphony of voices in narrative) lends his fiction great authority in challenging any one person's view of the world, inasmuch as that view asserts itself as theme.

Far better than E. L. Doctorow's *Ragtime*, which courts the opposite extreme by relegating history to the status of a character acting within the reader's memory, Reed's novels do not so much tell a story as generate a language in which historical events become signs, semiotic entities which in a grammatical fashion are allowed to be themselves even as they combine to form new meanings—meanings that derive their sense not by external reference but by pertinence to their own function in the author's composition. At one point in *The Terrible Twos* (New York: St. Martin's Press/Richard Marek, 1982), a futuristic novel which looks back upon the American present by reanimating its social and political signs in a new world brought into being by the narrative's constructions, the ghost of President Dwight D. Eisenhower appears to explain a little bit of the past:

> "If it hadn't been for Dulles," he cried. "That man had so much Bible and brimstone inside of him. The whole family—everybody but Allen was like him. They even had a fidgety woman preacher in the family. Dulles became haunted by that young black man. Said that when the young man, then a new leader of the Congo, visited Washington he sassed Dillon and the others. Swore up and down that Lumumba would bring the Communists to the Congo. Said that the Communism was the bitch of Babylon. Kept it up. Kept it up so much that I started smoking again, though I had sworn off the habit. And so one day, I was anxious to get out and play a couple rounds of golf at Burning Tree and they'd been pestering me all day about this Patrice Lumumba fellow, and so I stamped my foot and said, a guy like that ought to take a hike. I should have known when they started shaking hands and congratulating each other that something was up. I didn't mean for them to go and kill the man." (p. 112)

Unlike Robert Coover, whose *The Public Burning* employs classic American myths such as Uncle Sam and the Yankee pedlar in order to propose a contemporary fable, Reed takes signs as they are used in everyday life (in this case the media's image of the bewildered chief executive worried about old habits and eager for his golf game) to create a full-fledged fiction. As signs these factors can remain materially themselves, instead of being transformed by the myth-directed artist as transparencies for meaning—a structuring principle acknowledgment of the void disallows. The secretary of state's fundamentalist Christian fire, the African leader's presumed impertinence, the president's muddled confusion: these are not history itself but rather small icons once used as the lingua franca of the times, not as symbols of imposed meaning, and in Reed's fiction they contribute to the grammatical language of fiction.

Reed's transformation of history from fact to fictive tool squares with Ronald Sukenick's understanding of the novel's superiority.

Much as Norman Mailer's *Of a Fire on the Moon* acknowledges as source material not the NASA event itself but rather its structuralization as narrative by astronauts Neil Armstrong, Michael Collins, and Edward E. Aldrin, Jr. (and just as his *Marilyn* shares copyright with several other secondary accounts), Sukenick sorts out the differences between fact and fiction as outlined in his *In Form: Digressions on the Act of Fiction* (Carbondale: Southern Illinois University Press, 1985):

> The great advantage of fiction over history, journalism, or any other supposedly "factual" kind of writing is that it is an expressive medium. It transmits feeling, energy, excitement. Television can give us the news, but fiction can best express our response to the news. No other medium—especially not film—can so well deal with our strongest and often most intimate responses to the larger and small facts of our daily lives. No other medium, in other words, can so well keep track of the reality of our experience. (p. 242)

With Sukenick's fiction comes the critical vocabulary of postmodernism, as his work displays a combination of authorial intention and narrative action known as the *self-reflexive,* an interweaving of source materials and artistic creation called *intertextuality,* and a brash challenge to monological authority referred to as *dialogical.* Common to all three terms is an incorporation of the extraliterary in the act of fiction, a force that accommodates the world, not as an authenticating subject but as another text cited (think of Mailer's *Marilyn* if Sukenick's own *Out* and *98.6* seem too abstract), and that undermines the authority of order by showing how arbitrary and conventional (and subject to carnivalesque play) such orders are, particularly when we assume they come from the real world instead of from the writer's imagination.

The lessons Brautigan, Reed, and Sukenick strive to teach about fiction are ones learned almost a century earlier in painting, the art that often precedes the novel's innovation and gives it an aesthetic vocabulary. Just as Cézanne had separated the optical elements of experience from the conceptual, so do these writers sort out the constructive from the constituted; and as the Impressionist artist elaborates not so much on what is there as what he sees and how he sees it, the fictionist strives to efface content and privilege the structuring that is his or her part in acting. Before a painting is a bowl of apples, nude woman, or battle scene, it is a painting, a plane covered with colors and composed in a certain order; and with the need to represent a subject removed entirely, as the abstract expressionists found, the paint's action on the canvas could indeed become its own subject. Surely, the counterpoise of colors and textures in paint on canvas was as real as any subject matter that could be depicted, and moving directly to such counterposition rather than digressing through the form of a previously existing object could only enhance the nature of one's artistic act.

Not that such painting or such writing valorizes form as a principle or ideal toward which all else is made dependent. It is not the enduring but the momentary that matters in such works, the physical immediacy of real (and not recounted) experience. True, there are signs and symbols to be felt out (Brautigan's image of life in 1900, Reed's comic recollection of the president's 1950s image), but for readers the essence of experience remains in being entangled within the sensitizing process of narrative that turns out to be the message itself. If what has produced it is the artist's or writer's gesture, it is a gesture that lingers, like the graphic lines of a work by Cy Twombly (none of which means but all of which are sustained in a trace of their existence). It is the gesture that remains, not any product that it might otherwise indicate: gesture as the surplus of action, the action that has created the work. Born from the surface itself, the work (painting or narrative) finds its reality in the process of manipulation, not the object produced. Indeed, it is the graphic event that allows surface to exist at all.

Just as the major struggle in twentieth-century painting is between paint itself and what it becomes when applied to the canvas, so too does innovative fiction entertain the same distinction when it comes to the matter of its key element of composition. Is that element the word or the language that words form? In *Fiction and the Figures of Life* (New York: Knopf, 1970) novelist William H. Gass signals a radical break with conventionally (and unquestioning) realistic fiction by climaxing his argument with the linguistic nature of his medium:

> It seems a country-headed thing to say: that literature is language, that stories and the places and people in them are merely made of words as chairs are made of smoothed sticks and sometimes of cloth or metal tubes. Still, we cannot be too simple at the start, since the obvious is often the unobserved. Occasionally we should allow the trite to tease us into thought, for such old friends, the

clichés of our life, are the only strangers we can know. It seems incredible, the ease with which we sink through books quite out of sight, pass clamorous pages into soundless dreams. That novels should be made of words, and merely words, is shocking, really. It's as though you had discovered that your wife were made of rubber; the bliss of all those years, the fears . . . from sponge. (p. 27)

Gass is right, of course: we are indeed "so pathetically eager for this other life" (p. 37) that we tolerate all sorts of suspensions of disbelief in order to experience it vicariously, which is the substance of his novella about the sex-starved Willie Masters and the text that seeks his ravishment as a way of structuring its void. But Sukenick's complementary passage in *In Form* makes an important distinction:

Language is a self-contained system. Oui, monsieur. But the art of fiction and poetry lies precisely in opening that system up to experience beyond language. The obligation of fiction is to rescue experience from history, from politics, from commerce, from theory, even from language itself—from any system, in fact, that threatens to distort, devitalize, or manipulate. The health of language depends upon its contact with experience, which it both embodies and helps to create. The question is, "How can art open itself maximally to experience without destroying its integrity as artifact?" . . . The art field is a nexus of various kinds of energy, image, and experience. What they are, and how they interact, may in the long run be the most profitable area for criticism: the study of composition. (p. 11)

And so while Gass's fiction draws its substance from words—making them at times the very substance of his work, like Duchamp's shovel or urinal dropped into the context of art—Sukenick's novels and story collections find creative, compositional energy in the imaginative confrontations within the writer's life and the text which results from it, most often a text following the imperative to create the equivalent of a Watts Tower from that curiously intransitive verb, *to write*.

The key to such method is structuring the materials of fiction in ways which do not simply reflect a social phenomenology but which generate their own action. Such generation is found in the works of Stephen Dixon, Grace Paley, and Thomas McGuane, writers who share an activist use of signs. For them what would serve as a social notation in the hands of a *New Yorker* mannerist, projecting a counterfeit world too easily regressive into stale formulas and two-dimensional cutout shows reminiscent of the paintings of Alex Katz (of whom one of the magazine's minimalists, Ann Beattie, has published a major study), becomes instead an active work of art. Rather than depending upon a set of conventionalized references, Dixon uses the conventions to propel themselves through a story and situation until a self-supporting work is achieved, a remarkably satisfactory way of structuring his material without demanding a coherency of subject matter the postmodern world would deny.

Unlike the entropic styles and themes which from Pynchon to Beattie have found such favor with academic critics, Dixon's work is expansive rather than constricting, showing how within the range of familiar fictive techniques there remains a fresh world of discovery. His first stories collected in *No Relief* (Ann Arbor: Street Fiction Press, 1976) enlarge situations which would otherwise be limiting: breaking up with a lover, saying good-bye to a dying father, and having to explain to people how large such vacancies loom. His novels *Work* (Ann Arbor: Street Fiction Press, 1977) and *Too Late* (New York: Harper and Row, 1978) use the thematic routines of finding a job and searching for a missing loved one not as object lessons from the world but as structures for a narrative, structures that provide a vehicle for their ongoing strategy. One convention leads to another—not just in life, but in the texture of the literary work, which depends not upon any reference to life for its energy but rather upon the way Dixon lets one technique be prompted by and grow out of the other. *Work* shows how complete and complex a supposedly menial job can be, a virtual intertext of increasing considerations. *Too Late* confirms this method for his full-length fiction: how the simplest occasion, such as a girlfriend leaving a movie early, can lead to hundreds of pages of consequences, a style of casuistry that delights philosophers and drives neurotics mad, but which in the hands of a good novelist shows how rich the self-contained world of narrative can be. *Quite Contrary: The Mary and Newt Story* (New York: Harper and Row, 1979) follows this belief in interconnectedness and self-generation to its logical conclusion, that the story of a man and woman's relationship may fragment itself into an infinity of actions, yet will still cohere by virtue of its mutually attractive participants—a perfectly natural reinforcement of form and content, yet with no need for external verifiability. It's all an ocean, Dostoevsky exclaimed. For Dixon it's more like the logically connected but madly diverse Paris Métro, pulsing and aswirl with the evening rush that even though destined for the outside world (as words themselves must be) generates its own life of action.

Dixon's finest short stories are found in his three collections published by the Johns Hopkins University Press (Baltimore) in 1980, 1984, and 1990 respectively: *14 Stories, Time to Go,* and *All Gone.* Information—not data in itself but rather how it is used—fuels the stories in all three, as Dixon experiments progressively with interconnections in the present, interpenetrations of present and past, and the consequences of proceeding with interrupted or incomplete knowledge. All such motives are kept strictly within the text's bounds, with the result that these boundaries generate the possibilities of narrative. A suicide's bullet crashing through his hotel room's window and initiating other stories all around town, a son's and his fiancée's trip to the jeweler for wedding rings in the haunting presence of a lost father, the playing out of lives based on incomplete reports and mishandled information—the title stories of these three collections show how Dixon views limited themes and restrictive conventions not as inhibitions of expression but rather as invitations to write. The roots for such action are comic, as in "Love Has Its Own Action" (from *14 Stories*), where the event of a meeting and separation is replicated several times over, each time becoming faster and less contextually justified, until by the story's last paragraph the narrator is sundering old alliances and forging new ones at the rate of more than one per sentence. Yet there is ample chance for pathos as well as humor, as "The Sub" from this same collection demonstrates in its intricacies of fantasy and reality, all of them gestures over a content so simple as to be virtually nonexistent, a perfect occasion for structuring the void. A narrator crosses paths with a young woman and fills the story with his optatives and subjunctives for a shared success, a grammatical exercising of the only apparently real which climaxes with a run-through of what he could imagine happening after a first date—a date which, of course, never happens. Through the abundant detail, all of it projected rather than acted out, one sees how Dixon lets his narrator create a life out of the very conventions of syntax and verbal mood which other writers have found constricting, or which are used for counterfeit purposes of suggesting a supposedly real world. His story continues for twenty pages with all the techniques of realism, yet without their overriding and illegitimate purpose, for the narrator's conclusion is fully open-ended: "I think this will happen one day though I don't think the woman it will happen with will necessarily be her" (p. 53).

Stephen Dixon's manner of structuring the void thus encompasses Brautigan's, Reed's, and Sukenick's positions while not having to discard the materials of realism—Dixon simply alters their use and purpose, an approach that works equally well for both short stories and novels, indicating a transcendence of intrageneric distinctions that contributes to a new understanding of fiction itself. His massive 100,000 word novel, *Fall & Rise* (San Francisco: North Point Press, 1985), is generated by the same premise as "The Sub"—building a universal network of possibilities on the most passing (and least promising) of meetings with a total stranger. Here again the process of writing itself provides both structure and energy: the alternating fall and rise of action, of interest, and of narrative compulsion itself, just as in the rhythms of a writer's life, and completely different from both the metafictional display of the writing act which too often becomes the imitation of an imitation of an action and the opposite sense of proffering a report on the world.

Its plot is disarmingly simple, a reminder that structuring the void need not be an elaborate affair. At Diane's party Daniel meets Helene; he is taken with her and pursues her relentlessly through the few minutes of the party they share, even though she doesn't even notice. Daniel's compulsion to create a relationship matches the writer's drive to write, thereby textualizing the conventions of name, place, and date (and their context of social manners) which in the hands of a lesser talent, one in search of a formulaic shorthand for received attitudes, would escape the story to become extraliterary concerns. The book's seven chapters employ subtly differing styles as the action moves from the party itself to the park across the street, the street itself taking the focus uptown for a night's wanderings, and finally to Helene's apartment where in the early morning hours Daniel eventually seeks shelter. These narrative situations are aligned with the conditions of storytelling themselves, for as Dixon's narrator tries to take imaginative hold of his subject he must literally write himself into her life, while at the same time bearing responsibility for all the influences that intrude upon his own. The novel's action, spoken in his voice, is to incorporate her being, all from the slightest of provocations. Its present tense, which includes lots of dialogue registered in the same tone, speaks to the reader as another character. It is this influential sense of *presence,* of the narrative itself, that dominates the writing and stays with the reader long after the smaller details of plot, action, and character are forgotten. Not the presence of subject—Derrida and the other postmodern theorists have infinitely deferred that notion—but rather the presence of the writer/narrator's own endless network of possibilities, which as a self-contained system is created and sustained by the novel's own act of making fiction.

At each stage of *Fall & Rise* there are entire stories, from panhandlings to tavern squabbles to a robbery and mugging—narrative always has the possibility of breaking out anywhere. Pick up the phone and there's another story for Daniel, a mother's loneliness and vulnerability (the heat is out in her apartment), and any contact on the street invites a new dimension of activity. But structuring it all is Daniel's totally self-invented and self-sustained attempt to get Helene into his story—to get to her past bums and hoodlums, through her answering service and her doorman, until he's bedded down on her living room floor for what remains of the night (and the novel). It ends with Daniel still "writing" and the text still generating itself, a momentum halted only by Helene's sunrise invitation to have breakfast and depart. Her stopping of the narrative is the only way Daniel's story can end, just as the individual pieces in *14 Stories* are only halted by such patently mechanical devices as the narrator closing his eyes or someone else stepping in to guide his hand toward closure.

Dixon's much shorter novel, *Garbage* (New York: Cane Hill Press, 1988), is an even more insidiously compulsive narrative, beginning as it does with the most innocuous of encounters and not concluding until the action's entire context, the story's physical plant, is totally destroyed. Two men come into Shaney's bar and order beers, complimenting the narrator on his bartender's skill and looking for all the world like new steady customers. But within a page, the novel's first, their explanation of how they knew his name rings false, and by the third they're applying the rhetorical muscle of goons taking over the local refuse business. Shaney declines their services for no real reason beyond a textual consistency with himself: he likes his present hauler and sees no need to change. This obstinacy creates a resistance to the narrative's flow, an inexorable progress to the goal of the new garbage hauler moving in, and in succeeding pages it takes innumerable forms, from the pressure of the goons themselves to nuisances with the city health inspector, urgings from other bar owners who find it easier to change, and the disruption of Shaney's daily business and personal life. In this novel no chapter divisions are called for because the action is so quietly yet persistently continual; its first words have dealt with two apparently friendly guys coming in for beers, its last with the bar being destroyed in an apocalyptic end-it-all party Shaney organizes himself, with the 48,000 words in between devoted to the small steps of progression that move things from equilibrium to total disarray.

Because Shaney's posture as both narrator and protagonist is so evidently textual, he can generate an entire narrative simply by being himself, like a rock standing in a raging river and diverting the current even as it struggles to displace him. Similar in structural effect to *Fall & Rise*, *Garbage* achieves that effect by a passive rather than active approach: to structure his subject's void Dixon need only let his narrator/protagonist be himself, while the action fans out from its resistance to him. The former novel impels its story onward with the rhythm of breathing out and breathing in, the consequence of one action leading obversely yet completely to the next; only a blank page can end it, but even that blankness implies a world of language to be heard if the narrator can be allowed just one more word. Six words begin it ("I meet her at a party") and lead to another 100,000, each one spoken within the bounds of a coherent situation, in the present tense of an action filling the hours from 9 P.M. to daybreak with a world of possibilities generated by that initial sentence. *Garbage* achieves the same end by pursuing just the opposite strategy, as the narrator responds to its opening, "Two men come in and sit at the bar," by politely but resolutely trying to resist all such incursions into his stable world.

Similar variations on these approaches distinguish two of Dixon's strongest stories from these same years, "The Rescuer," first published in 1985 and collected in *The Play* (Minneapolis: Coffee House Press, 1988), and "Takes," a 1987 piece gathered into *Love and Will* (New York: Paris Review Editions/British American Publishing, 1989). Once again the complementary postures of being active and passive yield the same structural result, a strategy bound to work as long as those narrative stances remain pledged to the generation of a text rather than making hasty recourse to the verifiability of an outside world. "The Rescuer" uses the forwardly impelling present tense of *Fall & Rise* and

Garbage, beginning with "He hears people screaming, looks at them, looks where they're looking and pointing, and sees a child standing on a chair next to a balcony railing about ten stories up" (p. 110). Grammar and syntax set the form, which will move forward in short but compulsive leaps from one point of action to another—from looking at the people to looking at what they're looking at, a Chinese box structure whose form is made even more obvious by translating it into the linguistic terms that generate its power. Most of the story's succeeding paragraphs begin this same way and maintain the same effect.

"Takes" is equally consistent, but with a more concise, passively descriptive introduction: "Man's waiting in the service elevator right next to the passenger elevator" which begins the first paragraph, "Tenant on the eighth floor" starting off the second (p. 181), and so forth until the developing action is clear. Although both stories have a great amount of action, Dixon refuses to let that material serve as a subject or content in the traditionally realistic sense. Each is so terrifying (a child falling, a woman being raped and nearly murdered) that readerly attention might make either into a thing itself, rather than the proper void it is. Instead, the author structures his narratives with internally justified matters born of the text's action rather than just his characters'. In "The Rescuer" the protagonist is caught in a ceaseless narrative replication of the first page's act, while in "Takes" the victim, even as she drifts from consciousness and is taken to the hospital, remains a vital narrative feature in the stories of the man who has attacked her, the boyfriend who's dropped her off in a cab just before and is considering when to call her next, her mother in Connecticut worried over such dangers in New York, her roommate at a party downtown who, like the boyfriend and mother, wonders whether or not to call, and another tenant who has phoned the police and who—as among all of them the only one who has the slightest idea of what has happened—wonders if the young woman will survive. Each story seeks an absent content, even the subnarratives within "Takes"; each such seeking uses the writer's technique to structure a void.

Thomas McGuane and Grace Paley join Dixon in letting fiction's action grow naturally from its constituent materials—from its sign systems and contextual situations, the components that generate narrative action, rather than from motivation in the world they represent. The characters in McGuane's novels are often cast as readers of their culture, reacting less to its content than to its systems of semiotic communication. Consider the neo-Western cowboy hero of *Something To Be Desired* (New York: Random House, 1984), raised on personal-survival tales only to find his own adult life eclipsed by the stock lines people must speak in familiar situations. McGuane's protagonist comes home from a life not on the cattle trail but with the United States Information Agency during the turmoil of the 1960s and 1970s. He is pleased to note his experience "in an epoch when it seemed to him there actually were *signs,* an era in which he could join the rest of the populace in the wonderful ongoing melodrama of inanimate objects. He thrilled to clothes and cars; he sat at an old tropical wicker desk which seemed to guarantee character in his work" (pp. 149–50). Back home in southwestern Montana, he delights in the tacky residue of popular culture, including an early day drive-in that "should have been one of the primary artifacts, alongside the buffalo jumps and Calamity Jane's favorite bar, of this good little town" (p. 82). Seeing that so much of the world is manufactured, he tries to improve his own life, only to have this explicitly semiotic sense of "something better" spoil the casually achieved happiness he has been lucky to enjoy—another reminder that the writer's world of signs and the character's world of effects are two different realms indeed.

McGuane's own metaphor for structuring the void becomes the central image in *Keep the Change* (Boston: Houghton Mifflin/Seymour Lawrence, 1989), another novel of a postmodern Westerner struggling to regain his ranch heritage without sacrificing a consciousness that has grown beyond simple realism to a semiotically critical aptitude. In the series of such works McGuane has written on this theme, he poses his hero as returning from various professions; in this case the protagonist, Joe Starling, has been raised as a cowboy but has become famous as an abstract artist. The two roles are kept together throughout the narrative, beginning as it does with Joe as a boy, riding the high range with his father on a trip to see an old, abandoned home where one of the few remaining fixtures is a painting of subtle whiteness still hanging above the crumbling mantle. "When his own picture *Chain-Smoking Blind Man* had become known," he recalls, "only he was aware that its variegated white surface served against the canvas with a number-five putty knife was nothing more than his memory of the faded white hills on walls belonging to the long-dead Silver King and his spinster nieces. The feeling that he had invented nothing and that his career had begun with an undiscovered plagiary was disturbing" (p. 2). Yet through the perspective of Joe's consciousness an entire narrative has been created, one rich in language and complex in semiotic structure. At the end, when Joe visits the decrepit house for one last look at the painting, his closer inspection—as an adult and accomplished artist—reveals that his act has not been as a copyist but as a structurer of the void, because "There was no picture. There was a frame hanging there and it outlined the spoiled plaster behind it. It could have been anything. It was nothing, really. Close up, it really didn't even look like white hills. This of course explained why it had never been stolen. Joe concluded that no amount of experience would make him smart" (p. 214).

So much for how critical is subject matter as a thing in itself, as opposed to its *idea* (no thing in itself) as a generator of narrative. Grace Paley's fiction, often motivated by feminist concerns that would invite a more direct reliance on the world as subject, functions much the same as McGuane's work by using textually generated materials instead, and by doing so achieves a relevance to both political thought and postmodern literary theory. Like many other committed writers, Paley has devoted a certain portion of her work to issues of militarism, feminism, and social welfare. Yet her stories in *Later the Same Day* (New York: Farrar, Straus & Giroux, 1985) draw a picture of life seen not from a polemicist's platform but from an average woman's window, Paley's own version of the frame used in McGuane's *Keep the Change*. Her narrator in "Anxiety" shows this frame's importance when she uses it as a stage from which to warn a young father not to play too rough with his little girl, a warning that turns into much, much more:

> First I want to say you're about a generation ahead of your father in your attitude and behavior toward your child.
> Really? Well? Anything else, ma'am.
> Son, I said, leaning another two, three dangerous inches toward him. Son, I must tell you that madmen intend to destroy this beautifully made planet. That the murder of our children by these men has got to become a terror and a sorrow to you, and starting now, it had better interfere with any daily pleasure.
> Speech, speech, he called.
> I waited a minute, but he continued to look up. So, I said, I can

tell by your general appearance and loping walk that you agree
with me.

I do, he said, winking at his friend; but turning a serious face to
mine, he said, again, Yes, yes I do.

Well, then, why did you become so angry at that little girl whose
future is like a film which suddenly cuts to white. Why did you
nearly slam this little doomed person to the ground in your
uncontrollable anger.

Let's not go too far, said the young father. She *was* jumping
around on my poor back and hollering oink oink. (p. 101)

Paley's difference is to restrict her actual speeches to the PEN Congress and the White House lawn, while using her fiction to create a
character who is prompted to cry out against some specifically dangerous behavior and in the normal course of events relate it to the
greater issues of our world, yet in a manner generated by textual rather
than just political concerns. Note the absence of conventional punc-
tuation, forcing the reader to insert quotations, exclamation, and
question marks and so experience these lines as texts (virtually col-
laborating in the copyediting!) rather than simply ideas. Consider the
hopscotch movement among ideationally disparate notions (joys of
fatherhood, fears of nuclear war, hints of male chauvinism) which
make sense politically as a juxtaposition of emotionally fused issues.
And above all see the reliance upon metaphor—the film suddenly
cutting to white, a distance from the little girl and her life as broad as
any spanned by Richard Brautigan's structurings—as a way of expressing the obliteration of both a child's life and the planet's future in
one image reducible to neither event.

This is the peculiar sense of animation with which most of Grace
Paley's narrators speak, especially in her previous collection, *Enormous Changes at the Last Minute* (New York: Farrar, Straus & Giroux, 1974). Her women express themselves with a liveliness drawn
from their very material style of speech—"It is something like I am a
crazy construction worker in conversation with fresh cement" (p. 25),
one of them admits—because their energy comes from hands-on experience with the signs of life. She will have a drunken and enraged
husband wave a pistol before his eyes "as though it could clear fogs
and smogs" (pp. 113–14), and her protagonists (who are sometimes,
but not always, writers, and even then caught in tutorial conversations

with their traditionalist fathers) see all things graphically, from the sun setting as "a red ball falling hopelessly west, just missing the Hudson River, Jersey City, Chicago, the Great Plains, the Golden Gate— falling, falling" (p. 121) to the success of an immigrant father perceived before the American flag: "Under its protection and working like a horse, he'd read Dickens, gone to medical school, and shot like a surface-to-air missile right into the middle class" (p. 122).

As Dixon, McGuane, and Paley generate, Walter Abish celebrates. His own approach to extraliterary, outwardly referential materials is to surround and encompass them with his own identity as a writer, thereby taking the potential void of a subject matter and making it part of the writer's textual activity. Whereas doctrinaire postmodern theorists shun the autobiographical as outside the work, Abish turns this strategy inside out in order to textualize each event which has led to his present situation of putting pen to paper. In this way entire nations and epochs of history, from the Anschluss in Austria through the wartime and postwar transformations of China to the first years of the State of Israel, are no longer determining factors on the subject matter, or even subjects themselves; instead, Abish as the writer-to-be makes them serve his own cause of literary creation, thereby recuperating history on purely artistic terms within his own cause of literary creation.

"From the start," Abish asks in "The Writer-to-Be: An Impression of Living" (*Sub-Stance*, no. 27, 1980), "does the writer-to-be understand that his enterprise is in the nature of a quest, really a romantic quest for a number of interrelated things: (1) his text-to-be (2) the idea as well as the material for the text (3) his resolve to emulate and follow in the footsteps of the legendary heroes of writing: Hemingway, Miller, Thomas Wolfe, Kerouac etc. (4) and finally the quest for meaning. I mean by that the ontological search for an answer to the question: Why am I *I*, here, writing, thinking?" (pp. 101–2). Why should this act recuperate an otherwise outlawed subject matter? Because "The writer-to-be lives under the impression that everything, literally everything he experiences can be accurately transferred onto paper" (the allusion to photography is intentional) and that "for everything under the sun there is a corresponding sign or word, and that the intensity of his ardor, his passion for life, will impress upon the pages the determination of his new commitment" (p. 103). Note that the subject is not characterized as a representation to the reader, but as a factor in the writer's act. Creation is possession, and ultimately the writer possesses his or her world, a process the text celebrates as self: author, world, and writing as one. As with Dostoevsky's famous moment of reprieve, everything at once becomes possible: "I was crossing the parade ground in Ramale during my second year in the [Israeli] Tank Corps," Abish recalls, "when quite suddenly the idea of becoming a writer flashed through my mind. A moment of pure exhilaration" (p. 112).

Before the practice of exhilaration, however, come the moments of test. In his "Self-Portrait" from editor Alan Sondheim's *Individuals: Post-Movement Art in America* (New York: Dutton, 1977), Abish emphasizes how certain life experiences inhibit the text. "An individual will use language to give shape to his *I*" (p. 1), he begins, almost immediately adding that for even dead language, such as the cliché of *sink or swim*, there can be a challenge: "Having once almost drowned in a Shanghai swimming pool I cannot hear the word *or* mentioned without feeling a vague trepidation that is only somewhat assuaged when the speaker in question, out of compassion, says: Or else you can leave it the way it is" (pp. 5–6). Notice how it is the linguistic structure and not the word's referential quality that tests the writer's command of his art. It is the coordinating conjunction and not the art of swimming that he must master.

That mastery comes not by recounting experience in the conventional mode of autobiography but rather by textualizing the extraliterary, by making one's life a life of fiction. The pivotal example for Abish is in "Family" (*Antaeus*, no. 52, Spring 1984) where he examines "why things happened the way they did" (p. 149) by successively handling his parents' and his uncle's texts until, by virtue of the writer's work with language, they become his own—in other words, they become texts and not life, fiction rather than fact. And fiction, of course, is much easier to control, for here the writer is creator of his language rather than one created by it (through the events that have shaped it)— a nice variation of the intertextuality often said to shape involuntarily the writer's text. Looking back through this eminently controllable (because it is now retroactively viewable) past, Abish sees how his parents' style of living yielded freedom of choice for them but determination for him: "I was their product" (p. 151), he notes, and everything he did, mapped out in painstaking order, was simply to legitimize their role as the father and the mother of a child. Yet this function could be reversed, for "I was the only child. I was put there to observe them" (p. 152), and from this posture little Walter would become the writer-to-be, his observation literally textualizing events, making them perhaps an intertext for others but a controlled document for his own life:

> How could I possibly have known that I was being trained to be a writer? And that, in turn, my continuous attempts to break my mother's resistance were a preparation on my part to break down the resistance of the blank page I was to face years later. To break down the impediments of the text. Did they not see it? How could they have missed it? It was so obvious. My writerly concerns were, after all, printed all over my hideously distorted face. Deceit. Liar. A prig to boot. The price one pays if one is developing into a writer. (p. 152)

Growing up, Abish learns that his family's routines are rituals devised for understanding the outside world—for understanding history. As a child, he stands outside of history, but now, as an adult, he is faced with the challenge of making family history fit his own text (his own life) lest it swallow him entirely. Therefore he takes control, escaping the habits of "a world in which language served the supreme purpose of defining and interpreting conduct and planning the next day and the day after" (p. 153) and instead using language to textualize his extra-literary experience, thereby making it literary and hence malleable. The first step is to close off his free-running memories of family and stick to photographs, since they can be sorted, studied, arranged, and eventually shaped into a usable form. Then to find a manageable text: not just his memories of Uncle Phoebus, for example, which are prone to quandary and contradiction, but Phoebus's diary, where the "black-sheep" uncle himself had textualized experience, making "Each event a self-contained drama, a stage setting in which Phoebus . . . remains, despite his passionate language, the distanced observer of himself" (p. 161). Within these carefully framed tableaux there is "an almost painterly concern with the presentation of the event" (p. 162), anticipating Abish's writerly fascination with the otherwise historical detail from Phoebus's diary that is the uncle's sorrowful account of his brother Fritz's death, a problematic task which Phoebus handles textually by describing the brother's own diary. There are now three texts, successively enclosed within each other: Abish's which contains Uncle Phoebus's which contains Fritz's. Yet for the writer-to-be to become the writer-in-fact, Abish must learn to control texts, which means to edit. And so we see him putting one photo aside, "never show[ing] anyone," because it "seems to negate the role of black sheep I have applied to him" (p. 163), and concluding that he must discard another photograph that catches his parents in a casual, affectionate mood because "It invalidates everything I have described" (p. 169). What triumphs in the end is Abish's art of the text, since it transcends his uneasy memory of his parents' presumably artful lives, in which everything had to be deliberate—or so it seemed to little Walter. Where Abish has been able to textualize, life exists as fiction. Where he hasn't, there is "no trace" (p. 164) and therefore nothing effectively at all.

Abish's ultimate textualization of the extraliterary is found in his sequel, "The Fall of Summer" (*Conjunctions,* no. 7, 1985). Here the first person of "Family" yields to third-person narration, as Abish assumes the form of a character so he can more easily inhabit his text, now that its construction is assured. Autobiographically, Abish travels to West Germany for the very first time, after having imagined it in his novel *How German Is It* published the year before, and then returns to his native Austria—in particular, to the apartment building in Vienna where he lived for the first several years of his life, but which he now sees for the first time since 1938. Textually, he is well equipped to transpose the extraliterary into a literary form, for he has with him two guides: Thomas Bernhard's novel *Beton,* which he is savoring page by page and using as a kind of *Baedeker* so that "taste and not the 'story' " (p. 139) will shape his response, and the memory of a day ten years ago in the New York Public Library when he pored over the pages of a "profusely illustrated book by G. A. Jellicoe, an English landscape architect" (p. 136), by which he came to know the Belvedere's baroque gardens. Even though Abish was born in their proximity, he hadn't *known* the gardens until experiencing them through a readable text; hence his "one true moment of elation" (p. 136) on his first return visit comes when he can walk into not a memory but into a text now vitalized by his own participation in it. How anticipatory imagination (the literary) corresponds or fails to correspond to the actual subsequent experience is a familiar Romantic exercise, but in "The Fall of Summer" Abish finds that his goals demand the inversion of this structure, using the present experience to recapture a past moment of textuality. We now have a three-part process: memory of the 1930s which has been successfully textualized by a reading experience of the 1970s which in turn is vitalized by the writer's own physical participation in an event of the 1980s. True, as Dostoevsky says in the text's epigraph, "the world seemed to be created by me alone," and that "the whole world would dissolve as soon as my consciousness became extinct"; all would vanish "without leaving a trace behind" (p. 110). But Abish prefers to celebrate his conquest of the previously untextual by creating traces, the same traces Jacques Derrida values as the only possible form of postmodern presence in a world of structural absences—in other words the only acts by which we can structure the void.

In this process Abish's other extra-experiential guide—Thomas Bernhard's novel *Beton*—must have its own solution inverted. That work celebrates suicide as "a measure of life's energy . . . the energizer and guide in the text in which the 'ridiculous' is the sum of all human intercourse, all human exchange" (p. 111). Inverting Bernhard's formulation is how Abish becomes an American writer while Bernhard, by staying within such easy reach of home, remains the Austrian writer which Abish so firmly isn't. Outside of history as a child ("Family"), Abish textualizes the events in "The Fall of Summer" so that he can skip back over forty years of history to stand outside of it again: not because it hasn't happened, but because its happening has now been transformed into a text, a life of fiction where he is not just the writer-to-be but the writer-as-being. "Death is food for Bernhard," Abish notes. "He chews it thoroughly and comments on it. It is the food that replaces all need for sex" (pp. 111–12). Walter Abish, on the other hand, chooses life, with all its troublesome extraliterary dimensions (every one of them threatening to take command as a subject) because he has learned how to make them a successful part of his text. "Survival requires overcoming this resistance/opposition intrinsic to all things in everyday life" (p. 115), he has learned, from the resistance put up by his mother's fetishes of regimentation and expectation ("Family") to the opposition of the smothering, encompassing "familiarity" of a comfortable world (which has generated much of Abish's fiction and is what he rediscovers in Vienna—its constant temptation to take a short nap and dream away one's life in neat little pleasures, which is just how the world itself crushes the art of an unwary fictionist). Above all, there is the resistance of the page, what Ronald Sukenick's first essay in *In Form* describes as "The blank page, the void where everything is called into question" (p. 15).

Structuring the void, therefore, is motivated by the impossibility of writing any other way. As the notion of subject becomes suspect, fiction writers either develop a healthy fear for it or are devoured by it completely. Although the theory behind it comes from philosophy, its practice is eminently editorial, with the writers themselves becoming their own best critics. In an age when the vast majority of serious writers are college trained and employed as professors themselves, a situation encompassing not just the current crop of MFAs from the writing workshops but reaching back to Grace Paley's 1942 BA from Hunter College and current professorship at Sarah Lawrence, there is a studied professionalism that finds William H. Gass drawing on his doctorate in philosophy, Sukenick on his in English (a dissertation on the poetics of Wallace Stevens), and Abish spending as much time exploring the nature of his fiction writing as actually writing it.

Thus there is a clear awareness among these writers themselves of the issues behind the loss of subject matter in literary art. Yet such circumstances are neither surprising nor completely due to the influences of graduate degrees and college teaching. One hundred years ago fiction writers felt the same pressure from the world of ideas, as two generations of writers—the realists and then the naturalists—strove self-consciously to create a fiction in tune with the latest developments of philosophy and science (and in the process writing a number of serious critical tracts, including Zola's *The Experimental Novel,* Howells's *Criticism and Fiction,* and Norris's *The Responsibilities of the Novelist*).

It is when fiction not only lags behind but, through outdated commercial and academic standards, blocks the way for new work that today's writers launch their polemics. When Sukenick's *In Form* lodges the complaint that "The form of the traditional novel is a metaphor for a society that no longer exists" (p. 3), one need look no further for practical confirmation than to fellow novelist Gilbert Sorrentino's own collection of critical essays, *Something Said* (San Francisco: North Point Press, 1984). Sorrentino's career, much of it within the more progressive areas of commercial publishing (such as with Grove Press in the 1960s), extends Sukenick's arguments with form to the forms of traditional and innovative fiction, both of which are sarcastically deconstructed in his novel *Mulligan Stew.* Working with both editorial directors and authors, Sorrentino grappled with these forms not just as a writer but as an editor and advocate. His major project was Hubert Selby, whose work was an example of what in publishing had to be overcome: a commercial reliance on outmoded forms, a readerly disposition toward predictable styles, and the artistic temptation to surrender to such pandering. That Selby resisted all of this helped guarantee him both an original art and a career of frustration and rejection—to the extent that while his classic *Last Exit to Brooklyn* was being studied at the doctoral level in major European universities, Selby himself had to work pumping gas and cleaning windshields. Meanwhile, what sold commercially, especially to *The New Yorker,* was a fiction that solved the problem of incompatibility with subject matter by selling out art instead as a way of not only saving the referent but letting it do all the work, as Sorrentino explains:

> Some writers, the best, let's say, of the "popular writers," use clothing and "taste" as an indication of what to expect from the character. . . . [John] O'Hara will use a description of a vulgar character's tasteless clothes as an indication of that character's inherent vulgarity: the reader is clued as what to think. Occasionally, as if to show you that it's nothing but a gimmick, he'll write a story like "Exactly Eight Thousand Dollars Exactly": one character is held against another; the reader is given over to the movement of the story in terms of these characters' appurtenances and acts; and at the end, he turns the tables on you, a writer's joke. Which certainly indicates that he knows that these tricks are that, no more. (pp. 123–24).

As a writer's trick, such manneristic devices might be legitimate in a world whose viewpoint allows such clear correspondences between subject and technique. But when subject matter is itself suspect, it is the readers themselves who become manipulated and the writers who shirk their real duty:

> Signals in novels obscure the actual—these signals are disguised as conversation, physiognomy, clothing, accouterments, possessions, social graces—they satisfy the desire that we be told what we already know, they enable the writer to manipulate his book so that it seems as if life really has form and meaning, while it is, of course, the writer who has given it these qualities. It is the novel, of itself, that must have form; and if it be honestly made we find, not the meaning of life, but a revelation of its actuality. We are not

told what to think, but are instead directed to an essence, the observation of which leads to the freeing of our own imagination and to our arrival at the only "truth" that fiction possesses. The flash, the instant or cluster of meaning must be extrapolated from "the pageless actual" and presented in its imaginative qualities. The achievement of this makes a novel which is art: the rest is pastime. (p. 26)

The problem for readers is that "Such signals assure us that we are here, oh yes, in the world we understand," whereas what is being understood is not the world but the signals. But when proffered not as artifacts but as images of the real, such signals "allow the writer to slip out from under the problems that only confrontation with his materials can solve" (pp. 25–26).

Yet for all of the compromises with outdated literary technique, there remains a way to turn such signals to responsible postmodern use. Rather than employing them as a manneristic shorthand dependent upon the reader's acceptance of their referentiality, the fiction writer can seize the deconstructionist understanding of how reality is posed and exploit it for creative potential. Looking back on the first axiom that all such descriptions depend upon difference rather than identity, one recalls that understanding is therefore an ongoing process, a never ending succession of contrasts rather than definitions. The elements of such a process are as alive as art: interrelated by their distinctions rather than identities, they are characterized by their degrees of removal from the reality they would otherwise represent as subjects. These interactions deprive texts of ultimate external and immutable meaning, but thereby liberate those texts from slavery to an inevitable significance. The writer can now offer his or her own reality—the reality of his or her structurings—which in turn allows the text to create the new. The resultant system literally structures the void, because the play of differences which makes up the system is inscribed not in the final product but in each of its constituent elements, with each element in itself being constituted by virtue of this inscription. The system and its play are organized not by a represented subject but by a principle that is both within and without it. Most importantly, there is none of the immobility and certitude of a subject, but rather just the trace of difference appearing in every other difference which together conveys a notion of structuring the void. There is no origin of meaning such as a subject would convey—just the activity of each part existing by virtue of the other.

It is this view of the world (and our role in it) that has led fiction writers from Richard Brautigan in the 1960s to Stephen Dixon in the 1990s to devise ways of generating narratives not from reference to a subject but from their own acts of structuring. In their hands what would want to be a subject, and thus be swallowed up by the void of indefinability, is transformed into an occasion for activity surrounding that void. Gilbert Sorrentino's dual appreciation of how a social mannerist like John O'Hara devised an art of signals only to have successive generations take an easy way out by substituting signals for things holds out the promise that the process can be once more reversed, and that signs might once again be recognized for what they are: not identities but things in themselves, things that achieve meaning only in a network of differential relationships.

Such relationships risk hasty identifications with the familiar world, making it dangerous for the writer to propose them. Yet when these signs are not commodities in the great social world but rather elements of one's own identity, the writer has a more apparent chance for control—especially when, as in the case of Kurt Vonnegut, those elements are used not just for shaping an autobiography but for structuring a world of experience that without them threatens to be an ineluctable void.

For these purposes, Vonnegut's example is an ideal one. His fiction reinvents the genre even as the world he faces, in its rush toward the twenty-first century, demands redefinition in terms of the previously unthinkable terms which have, since 1945, become part of its nature. As his characters are fond of stating, one can look back to any of the greatest literary masterpieces of earlier ages and appreciate their achievement, yet also understand that for postmodern times such representations are no longer sufficient. From *Player Piano* and his short stories of the early 1950s to his fiction of the 1990s, Vonnegut proposes a uniquely systematic response, generating an interrelated narrative that defines itself not in reference to an outside world but in terms of its own act of structuring. Once accomplished, such work may not efface the void of an incomprehensible world, but it certainly suggests what may be counterposed against it. As such, it becomes one of the chief examples for subsequent writers, who from this biographical base move on to study the structuring powers of such self-made systems as ritual, comedy, game, play, and even such determinants as gender, warfare, and the spatial nature of the artifacts we build. But first comes the need for a thorough understanding of the structuring nature of autobiography, for which Vonnegut's has been the work of genius.

2

Biography:

Kurt Vonnegut's

America

If the subject is in doubt, at least the self can be known, at the very minimum of knowing that one's self exists. This notion might seem simple to the point of being simplistic. But like so many other factors in Kurt Vonnegut's work, it is a simplicity that assumes nothing and thus avoids the postmodern dilemma of everything being put into question. From his first novel Vonnegut assumes nothing, beginning in almost schoolboy fashion by mimicking the one classical text old-fashioned students might be expected to know—Caesar's *On the Gallic War*, the first words of which (with only the lateral substitution of "Ilium" for "Gaul") serve quite adequately as not only an introduction to the narrative of *Player Piano* but an indication of its structure as well. Vonnegut's quintessential postmodern industrial town is divided into three parts—for the engineers, workers, and machines respectively—and from this triadic form derives just about everything that follows. Yet for the author himself what makes the tale coherent is that for all its dystopian qualities the story corresponds to his own experience in the very real triadic metropolis of Schenectady-Albany-Troy (respective homes of the machines, workers, and engineers) during the postwar period when such factors became a structural principal of American life.

These are the two constants that run through Vonnegut's work: Vonnegut himself and the America he has lived in since his birth in 1922. That he did not achieve recognition until the late 1960s indicates the innovative nature of this approach, for nearly two decades of cultural transformation would be needed until such novels as *Player Piano, The Sirens of Titan, Mother Night,* and *Cat's Cradle* could be read compatibly within our understanding of the times; written in the age of John O'Hara, it would take the age of Richard Brautigan to fully understand and accept them as its own. Yet in the most fundamental sense, Vonnegut's canon was a revolution just waiting to happen, as for the most part his thinking grew out of the solid, middle-class heritage most of his countrymen share.

The key to his literary revolution is that in both his fiction and his journalism Kurt Vonnegut found a way of taking events—even the fantasies of science fiction and the calamities of recent national history, most of them so unconventional as to deny expressibility as subject matter—and measuring them against the mundane, stable facts of his own American life. His happy childhood in a large family in the Midwest, his study of science (during its heyday) at college, his fraternity life, his service in World War II, his study under the GI Bill after the war, his public relations work for a giant corporation, and his own large and growing family—these experiences, which can easily be duplicated in the lives of perhaps a million men his age, have been fashioned by Vonnegut into a personal system by which he measures the world. Because its sources are so common, it becomes a system for America itself, which is the principal reason why his works are so popular.

Vonnegut grew up in the Great Depression, an experience that shaped both his life and his fictional style. When he was still young enough to modify his notions of reality, young Kurt saw his entire world transformed. His father, a second-generation architect and member of a socially and artistically prominent family, went ten years without a commission because of the dearth of building projects. His mother, who had grown up in the comfortable wealth of the Lieber brewing fortune, was subjected to the humiliation of selling her family crystal and china. The Vonneguts had to give up their beautiful home for a more modest house. Twenty years later, when his father died, Kurt turned to the Depression in an unfinished novel titled *Upstairs and Downstairs*. Its plot centers on the economic hardships of the narrator's family, which force them to rent the upstairs of their home to an eccentric businessman named Fred Barry (who will appear many years later in *Breakfast of Champions*). One of Fred's quirks is to give the narrator a wallet with six hundred dollars. "And in those days you could have bought the moon for six hundred dollars. That was nineteen thirty-six." Fred makes him keep the money "for a whole day, just to see what having that much money felt like." Money, of course, can transform one's world, just as the lack of it had changed the boy's world in the story. How money, or other things, can absolutely change one's idea of reality was a theme that Vonnegut would explore in every one of his novels from *Player Piano,* written during his spare time while working as a publicist for General Electric, to *Hocus Pocus,* the masterwork of one of the world's most famous writers.

The Depression also served to move Vonnegut out of Indianapolis, his family's home for three generations, to begin the migration that would carry him far from his Indiana roots. Urged by his father to study something "useful," he undertook majors in biology and chemistry at Cornell University, leaving Indianapolis in 1940, never to live there again.

But from his Indiana years Vonnegut took two precious gifts: the ideals of his family and the humor of radio and film comedians of the Depression era. "When people ask me who my culture heroes are," he wrote in the preface to *Between Time and Timbuktu* (New York: Delacorte Press/Seymour Lawrence, 1972), "I express pious gratitude for Mark Twain and James Joyce and so on. But the truth is that I am a barbarian, whose deepest cultural debts are to Laurel and Hardy, Stoopnagel and Bud, Buster Keaton, Fred Allen, Jack Benny, Charlie Chaplin, Easy Aces, Henry Morgan, and so on. They made me hilarious during the Great Depression, and all the lesser depressions after that" (p. xvii). His novel *Breakfast of Champions* (New York: Delacorte Press/Seymour Lawrence, 1973) is dedicated to "Phoebe Hurty, who comforted me in Indianapolis—during the Great Depression"; Mrs. Hurty, a forty-year-old widow, supervised the witty ad copy Vonnegut wrote for the Indianapolis *Times* and the commercial advertisers in the high school newspaper he edited and was the inspiration for his bawdiness and lack of respect for the sacred cows of our culture, an attitude she believed would shape a new American prosperity and which her protégé used as the stylistic base for his self-created world.

Although the firebombing of Dresden is usually considered the most traumatic event in Vonnegut's life, both as a writer and as a person, he himself considers the Great Depression to have been a far more difficult ordeal for the country as a whole. What palliated it were the little daily doses of humor from the comedians, most of whom had weekly radio shows; such encouragement and relief served to make things bearable and even understandable—not through complicated explanations, but by redefining the system's terms so as to make mankind lovably foolish rather than vexingly culpable. Later on Vonnegut found the same appeal in the work of Bob and Ray, Bob Elliott and Ray Goulding, whose *Write If You Get Work* (New York: Random House, 1975) he prefaces with an appreciation of their art: "While other comedians show us persons tormented by bad luck and enemies and so on, Bob and Ray's characters threaten to wreck themselves and their surroundings with their own stupidity. There is a refreshing innocence in Bob and Ray's humor. Man is not evil, they seem to say. He is simply too hilariously stupid to survive. And this I believe" (p. vii). Vonnegut's own novel *Slapstick* (New York: Delacorte Press/ Seymour Lawrence, 1976), which the author describes in its prologue as an autobiographical compendium of his personal beliefs, is dedicated to the film comedians Laurel and Hardy. His life, Vonnegut says, "is grotesque, situational poetry—like the slapstick film comedies, especially those of Laurel and Hardy, of long ago." This is what life feels like to him, the author insists, with all its "tests of my limited agility and intelligence. They go on and on." What Vonnegut admires in Laurel and Hardy is "that they did their best with every test. They never failed to bargain in good faith with their destinies, and were screamingly adorable and funny on that account" (p. 1).

The great popular comedians of the American 1930s gave Vonnegut the basis for his artistic style—short statements of alternating situations and problems, capped by a punch line that undercuts their premise (and their seriousness)—and his central beliefs come from an equally humble source: the lessons of his parents and schoolteachers from the same period. Throughout the heyday of his fame as a guru of disaffected youth during the great countercultural protests of the late 1960s and early 1970s, Vonnegut was fond of disarming interviewers with the answer that all his supposedly radical beliefs could be traced to the civics classes he was taught in grade school and high school and that pacifism itself was a national ideal in the 1930s.

Throughout high school and college Vonnegut found himself responding to events as a writer, working as he did as managing editor of the Shortridge *Echo* and the Cornell *Sun*. Being away at college made him lonesome for the great extended family of parents, aunts, uncles, and cousins he had enjoyed in Indianapolis, but also taught him that such circumstances could be restructured artificially: through the brotherhood of fraternity life. Then came service in the war, with further lessons about the great mischief that could result from taking national identity too seriously (as an absolute rather than an arbitrary factor, just as fraternity skirmishes sometimes get out of hand), followed by more organized study of the nature of humankind as a graduate student in anthropology at the University of Chicago. At Chicago Vonnegut investigated what it takes to form a revolutionary group (his thesis proposal, comparing the Cubist painters with the Plains Indians' Ghost Dance Society, was rejected for daring to mix civilized and primitive cultures) and then moved on to analyze the distinctive structures of narratives according to their sources (a technique he'd exploit in coming years with short stories for the various popular magazines). Finally there was more writing, but none of it in the rarefied realm of the serious novel. Instead, Vonnegut practiced his trade as a pool reporter for the Chicago News Bureau, as a publicist for the General Electric Research Laboratory in Schenectady, New York, and ultimately as a free-lance writer selling short stories to *Collier's, Argosy,* and *The Saturday Evening Post.* Along the way he was following the course taken by countless other veterans: returning to marry a childhood sweetheart, getting some college on the GI bill, going to work for one of the big American corporations whose acronyms were spelling out the country's future, and eventually moving into a small trade or business of one's own (in Vonnegut's case producing stories to specification for the family magazine market). It was only when his chosen business hit a slump and (with the demise of *Collier's* and the *Post*) began to fall apart that Vonnegut began to apply his major effort to the writing of novels.

Those novels, it turns out, look back to the principal events of his life not for their subject matter—for Vonnegut would be among the first to discard a coherent subject as material necessities—but as structuring devices, the makings of a system by which otherwise inexplicable postmodern phenomena could be handled in a comprehensible narrative. That these components were his major autobiographical experiences made the method conform to deconstructive practice on both sides: as a view of the world composed not of identities but of difference (not atomic holocaust, for example, but rather contrasts between it and factors the author had encountered at home, at Cornell, and in Chicago) and as an understanding of the self per se but only as his own adventures within language and its play of difference (ultimately traceable as Heidegger's being-in-the-world).

Yet before the novels would break through to a large and apprecia-tive reading public (and before Vonnegut would in turn break through to a triumph of autobiographical method in *Slaughterhouse-Five*), there remained one more field in which to work. By 1965, with his short story markets dried up and his novels garnering either low-paid virtual anonymity as paperbacks or as poor selling hardcovers, Von-negut undertook one last style of applied writing: that of feature journalism. After a year or so of doing book reviews for the *New York Times Book Review* and *Life*, he began publishing highly personalized essays in the *New York Times Sunday Magazine*, *Life*, and *Esquire*, most of which have been collected in *Wampeters, Foma & Gran-falloons* (New York: Delacorte Press/Seymour Lawrence, 1974). His topics are nothing new, and serve less as subjects than as occasions for him to generate narratives from his autobiographical system, compar-ing such wonders as the Maharishi Mahesh Yogi, the Apollo 11 moon launch, a mass murderer on Cape Cod whom the media had turned into a superstar, the peculiar nature of the Nixon Republicans govern-ing America, and dozens of other topics close to the daily lives of his countrymen to things that had happened to him as long ago as his childhood in Indianapolis. His attitude was much the same as his stories of the 1950s: extolling middle-class virtues and ridiculing the pretensions of the rich and powerful. Vonnegut admitted that he wanted to watch an Apollo launch because its very spectacle struck his little-boy fancy with firecracker explosions. His piece on the Mahari-shi carried the title "Yes, We Have No Nirvanas," and the Maharishi's appeal was shown to be just another product to feed middle-class consumerism. After attending a Transcendental Meditation session with the leader, Vonnegut came away irked by the movement's blithe-some ease and mundane practicality. "I went outside the hotel after that," he writes, "liking Jesus better than I had ever liked Him before. I wanted to see a crucifix, so I could say to it, 'You know why You're up there? It's Your own fault. You should have practiced Transcendental Meditation, which is easy as pie. You would also have been a better carpenter" (pp. 40–41).

These essays featured the same development that was becoming evident in Vonnegut's fiction during these years: the ability to treat his subject by making himself the center of it and then reporting on himself. It was the method of the New Journalism, made popular about this time by Tom Wolfe, Hunter S. Thompson, Dan Wakefield, and many others. As a device it popularized Vonnegut's personality, which remained as ruggedly simple as ever, especially when confronted with an alien subject. Asked to review the Random House Dictionary for the *New York Times Book Review,* Vonnegut produced a piece sufficiently artistic and imaginative to be collected with his short stories in *Welcome to the Monkey House* (New York: Delacorte Press/Seymour Lawrence, 1968). His approach is to put the lexicographer's terms into simple English, the English spoken by people who had shared lifetime experiences similar to his. "Prescriptive," Vonnegut wrote, "as nearly as I could tell, was like an honest cop, while descriptive was like a boozed-up war buddy from Mobile, Ala." (p. 108). The trick here is not only to be wildly comparative, anticipating the great distances between tenor and vehicle in Richard Brautigan's metaphors and similes, but to familiarize the rather abstract tenor (given to the author in his review assignment) by searching out a vehicle from a common fund of mundane experience the author and reader share. In this way, both the alien topic and the person who must explain it exist solidly within the reader's familiar world.

Just about everything Vonnegut saw in his role as journalist was reduced to simplicity, but in a homely, charming way. During his years on Cape Cod he had lived just across the peninsula from Hyannis; among his neighbors were the household employees of the fabulous Kennedy family. Now, with the Kennedys being further glamorized by the world press, Vonnegut was able to sell an essay to *Venture* describing a trip taken with Frank Wirtanen, skipper of their yacht. But instead of flattering the Kennedy vessel (and being flattered by it) he chose to point out its humble realities. During the summer most of its service was as a playground for the Kennedy children and their friends:

> The *Marlin*'s captain, Frank Wirtanen of West Barnstable, Cape Cod, says of his present duties, "I don't think a man without children of his own, without a real understanding of children, could hold this job very long without going bananas."
> Captain Wirtanen is a graduate of the Massachusetts Maritime Academy. He used to command tankers, both in peace and in war. He now has the Kennedy yacht fitted out with a system of rubber mats and scuppers that make it possible for him to hose away the remains of chocolate cake and peanut-butter-and-jelly sandwiches in a fairly short time. (*Wampeters,* p. 8)

The journey for Vonnegut's readers here is just as extensive as in his similes devised for the dictionary review, for Kennedy glitter is dimmed into a most familiar complaint about children, one's *own* children (as the reader is asked to appreciate), while Captain Wirtanen's career is followed from the equal extremes of evading killer submarines on the Atlantic convoys to hosing away cake crumbs and sandwich crusts. At the far pole, of course, is something his audience has known only through glamorous imagery, and so Vonnegut works to relate it to his and his readers' everyday lives.

Throughout these essays, as in his novels, Vonnegut has measured the whole world by his own private standards: growing up in Indianapolis, going off to college and war, working for General Electric, and fashioning his own middle-class life in the village of West Barnstable, Massachusetts. His journalistic writing gave him the chance to organize his own interpretive system before dealing with the biggest event in it: the firebombing of Dresden, which he witnessed as a prisoner-of-war.

The true achievement of *Slaughterhouse-Five* was that, after twenty years of trying to write about it, Vonnegut finally realized that the truth of his Dresden experience was not the firebombing itself but his own reaction to it. To a student audience at the University of Iowa in 1969 he described just how elusive Dresden was as a subject and how it would be his own structuring of this void that produced the novel:

> Anyway, I came home in 1945, started writing about it, and wrote about it, and wrote about it, and wrote about it. This thin book is about what it's like to write a book about a thing like that. I couldn't get much closer. I would head myself into my memory of it, the circuit breakers would kick out; I'd head in again, I'd back off. This book is a process of twenty years of this sort of living with Dresden and the aftermath. It's like Heinrich Böll's book, *Absent Without Leave*—stories about German soldiers with the war parts missing. You see them leave and return, but there's this terrible hole in the middle. That is like my memory of Dresden, actually there's nothing there. I'm pleased with it. (Joe David Bellamy, ed., *The New Fiction: Interviews with Innovative American Writers* [Urbana: University of Illinois Press, 1974, pp. 202–3])

As Vonnegut would explain in many other interviews, massacre on such a huge scale—the Dresden casualties were measured as high as a quarter million from the single raid—simply does not register with the mind. He had been reminded of the same lesson when writing about mass-murderer Tony Costa on Cape Cod and when reporting on the mass starvation engineered in Biafra: some atrocities are simply too large for the human imagination to grasp. As a result, people shrink away from such happenings or excuse them with a nervous giggle; and since the reality of mass murder is never absorbed, it is never understood, and thus cannot be prevented from happening again. But rather than losing the subject entirely, or—even worse—writing a detached account glorifying the adventure of war, Vonnegut kept it in front of him, unexpressible as it was, by detailing his attempts to face it. The result was *Slaughterhouse-Five*.

The importance with which Vonnegut regarded this role of structuring the void is evident not only in the way he has conducted himself since becoming famous, which is to remain active as a public spokesman on political, social, and ecological issues (many of which are so complex as to boggle the imagination), but also from comments on the importance of fiction in his earlier novels. Anthropological training and firsthand experience in seeing his family's reality transformed by the Great Depression had convinced him that reality was something arbitrary and impermanent, since the basic facts of life could be changed by circumstances of birth or by the whims of national economics even after one was half-grown. But while other writers might find such conditions to be the basis for a pessimistic or even hopeless determinism, Vonnegut used his ingenuity to turn them around as the components of humankind's true freedom. If reality is indeed relative and arbitrary, then it is all the easier to change; men and women need not suffer an unhappy destiny, but can instead invent a new one better suited to their needs. In *Slaughterhouse-Five* (New York: Delacorte Press/Seymour Lawrence, 1969) we are told that because of the horrors of war, Billy Pilgrim and Eliot Rosewater "both found life meaningless"; therefore, "they were trying to re-invent themselves and their universe. Science fiction was a great help" (p. 87).

Writers, by virtue of their ability to structure a void rather than surrender to it, should be the first change makers, Vonnegut's novels argue. As a philanthropist, Eliot Rosewater had shown a convention of science fiction writers just how arbitrary one cornerstone of our reality, money, is—thus empowering them to undertake the reinvention he and Billy Pilgrim will eventually seek. His example, in *God*

Bless You, Mr. Rosewater (New York: Holt, Rinehart and Winston, 1965) is to write a $300 check for each of them as an act of whimsy. "Think about the silly ways money gets passed around now," Rosewater tells them, "and then think up better ways" (p. 31). Such transformations of reality might then be translated from the aesthetic to the ethical and social spheres—as Kilgore Trout suggests at the end of *Rosewater,* and as Bokonon and McCabe accomplish for a time in *Cat's Cradle* (New York: Holt, Rinehart and Winston, 1963). The two of them "did not succeed in raising what is generally thought of as the standard of living" on San Lorenzo, we are told. "But people didn't have to pay much attention to the awful truth. . . . They were all employed full time as actors in a play they understood, that any human beings anywhere could understand and applaud" (p. 144).

As for personal worth, Vonnegut turned again to his extended family, rich in generational traditions, in Indianapolis, and to what he studied in the University of Chicago's anthropology program. The need for primitive folk societies would become his major topic following Dresden, beginning with his play *Happy Birthday, Wanda June* in 1970 (where involvement with the production's theatrical community replaced the loss of his grown-up and departed family on Cape Cod) and culminating with his novel *Slapstick.* Both involve artifice; but as culture is not a bedrock reality, but only a description, why not come up with a more usable description once the old one has lost its efficacy? In the 1970s, empowered as a famous writer, Vonnegut can be found doing the same things in his life as in his fiction: proposing new definitions for not only happiness but for survival.

As Kurt Vonnegut's values are derived from the common practices of middle-class American life, the themes and structures of his novels reflect his own autobiography within this same social, political, and cultural context. From *Player Piano* to *Hocus Pocus* he charts a steady course through not just the influences but also the specific experiences of his lifetime in the United States—as a child in one of its Midwestern cities, a student in its grade school and high school civics classes, a college student learning about the brave new world of science and technology (as examples of American "know-how" set to reinvent the world), a soldier defending his country abroad (and, at Dresden, seeing the technology he'd only recently studied unleashed to destroy a cultural treasure), a GI-bill educated veteran setting off to build a career in one of its great postwar corporations, a small businessman manufacturing and selling his wares to a wide distribution network (in this case short stories to the family magazines), and finally one who has emerged as a leading novelist, whose position as a spokesman for larger causes would lead him to be styled as a great public writer in the manner of Mark Twain—another example of the formative power of the vernacular experience.

His first novel, *Player Piano* (New York: Scribners, 1952), begins with a paean to good old American "know-how" (p. 1) for having won what his fictional construct projects as World War III—for this is to be a story of utopia, set several decades hence in the future. Yet that future turns out to be modeled quite faithfully on the past, including all of the foibles that have characterized the less successful aspects of American history, including the diminution of aesthetic and spiritual values in the service of a higher material standard of living. A technological miracle has allowed the nation to achieve maximum production with minimal, almost nonexistent manpower—a boon when those who would otherwise be workers are off fighting at the front, but a problem when those millions return home and find nothing to do. To address these issues Vonnegut draws on not just his experience as a publicist for the General Electric Corporation's Research Laboratory, but on his postgraduate training at the University of Chicago, giving one of his spokesmen, the Reverend James J. Lasher, an M.A. degree in anthropology. With the First Industrial Revolution making manual labor redundant, and the Second discounting routine mental work, the Third Revolution at hand—the age of computers whose thought capacity outranks that of the brightest human—discounts creativity and imagination themselves, to the extent that "what's left is just about zero" (p. 35). From Vonnegut's undergraduate and army instruction in science and engineering comes another dimension of *Player Piano*'s analysis, as offered by the character Dr. Paul Proteus, a nominal leader of this revolution but whose spiritual malaise prompts him to take part in a counterrevolt against the machines and all they imply. Yet Paul's cause is a hopeless one, for it runs against the grain of a key American trait: "the restless, erratic insight of a gadgeteer" that has created the present state of affairs, "a climax, or close to it . . . with almost all of American industry integrated into one stupendous Rube Goldberg machine" (p. 36). What makes this machine unique, however, is that it is programmed to self-destruct.

Yet it is the narrative itself that shows a commonly American middle-class character, and it is this attitude that stamps the book as Vonnegut's own. The narrative stance of *Player Piano* is third-person omniscient, but no novel can note everything. There's an idiosyncratic style to what Vonnegut selects, and it follows the pattern of his popular essays and feature journalism written decades later. When covering the Apollo moon launch for The *New York Times Magazine* (the piece collected as "Excelsior! We're Going to the Moon! Excelsior!" in *Wampeters, Foma & Granfalloons*), he'd begun with a disarming statement: despite the high technology and epic nature of the occasion, he had come down to Florida for the same reason he'd loved to shoot off fireworks as a kid—to hear the big bang of ignition and lift-off. The attraction of such events is the sound, and in *Player Piano* Vonnegut's omniscient narrator approaches the technological miracle of automation the same way:

> At the door, in the old part of the building once more, Paul paused for a moment to listen to the music of Building 58. He had had it in the back of his mind for years to get a composer to do something with it—*the Building 58 Suite*. It was wild and Latin music, hectic rhythms, fading in and out of phase, kaleidoscopic sound. He tried to separate and identify the themes. There! The lathe groups, the tenors: *"Furazz-ow-ow-ow-ow-ow-ak! ting! Vaaaaaaa-zuzip!"* And, with the basement a resonating chamber, the punch presses, the basses: "Aw-grumph! tonka-tonka. Aw-grumph! tonka-tonka . . ." It was exciting music, and Paul, flushed, his vague anxieties gone, gave himself over to it. (p. 10)

Paralleling Vonnegut's later comparison between a Saturn rocket lift-off and a child's play with fireworks is *Player Piano*'s association of the Ilium Works' technological symphony with the sound of the washing machine at home, whose comforting *urdle-urdle-urdle* plays counterpoint to the harsher sounds from the machines in Building 58. In each case mechanical marvels are reduced to the infantile sounds that fascinate the primitive interests of their human beholder—once again a reduction of the most complex and exotic properties to the most basic dimension possible.

Player Piano's narrative perspective takes the same approach to social themes. Counterpointing the futuristic action at the General Forge & Foundry is the visit of an Asian religious leader, the Shah of

Bratpuhr, who is touring the Works for an introduction to the miracle of American efficiency. Although simple narrative omniscience would include the privilege of understanding his language, the novel gives us a transcription of the Shah's native tongue in advance of translation— partly for the apparently nonsensical music of his strange language (sounding much like another machine from the Building 58 symphony), but mostly for the humor in showing how what first seems like something special turns out to be as familiar as apple pie. Lines like *Brahous brahouna, houna saki* are intermixed with others such as *Puku palo koko, puku ebo koko, nibo aki koko,* and in their native state imply great profundity. But Vonnegut's narrative quickly teaches the need for discrimination, based on a healthy skepticism that delights in the difference between the first sentence, which encapsulates the mystically incantatory greeting of the Kolhouri religion, and the second, a series of instructions to the barber that read "a little off the sides, a little off the back, and leave the top alone" (p. 175), probably the most common message in any American barbershop at the time, especially as it prompts an equally banal line of chatter from the barber who rattles on with pointless comments about politics, sports, and the weather, regardless of the Shah's or any other customer's ability or willingness to listen. In this way the mechanical opera of industrial machines and housewives' washers makes about as much or as little sense as human palaver. Indeed, many of the novel's lines of dialogue are cast as maddening repetitions, from the inevitable greeting Paul gets from people seeing him drive up the street ("Hey, Mac, your headlight's busted!") to the inevitable interchange with his wife, whose "I love you, Paul" allows for no other possible response than the mechanically automatic "I love you, *too,* Anita."

Vonnegut thus molds *Player Piano* in the shape of his own personality, even though so many of his later stylistic techniques are yet to be in evidence: no exceptionally short chapters, paragraphs, or sentences, no cynically barbed examples of black humor (although a pompous technocrat is found to have a deficiency on his college transcript and is sent back for a grueling physical education class), and no appearance within the text of the author himself (although the character Reverend Lasher seems to have proposed the same master's thesis, on the anthropological consequences of the Plains Indians' Ghost Dance Society of the 1890s, as did Vonnegut himself). That this molding takes place by means of narrative voice itself speaks for the strong foundation of

Vonnegut's vision, which here as always is based on his own auto-biographical experiences within the most familiar aspects of American middle-class life.

When his second novel takes off for a moon of the planet Saturn, this familiarity of Vonnegut's vision faces an even stronger test than the only moderately futuristic dystopia of *Player Piano.* Yet much of *The Sirens of Titan* (New York: Dell, 1959) exists in order to make ironic comments on its own theme and structure, which are the foibles of human greed and vanity within the format of low-grade science fiction space opera. With a previous novel and nearly three dozen family magazine stories under his belt, Vonnegut can begin including himself within his fiction by making some sly intertextual references, such as when invaders from Mars are disguised as familiar figures from the author's own canon, "two *Saturday Evening Post* characters at the end of the road" (pp. 86–87), a doubly ironic reference since Vonnegut was turning to novel writing again only because his markets for stories at the *Post* and *Collier's* were drying up. But the larger strategy of *The Sirens of Titan* is to undercut human pretensions by shooting holes in one of its most popular literary forms. Space opera is an example of the arrogance of human control: feeling that one can write confidently about the future by using the most shabbily contemporary aspects of popular life. In such works heroes look and act like the cowboy-novel protagonists of old, while their women are a combination of frontier dance-hall entertainers and modern dreamgirls—hence the term space opera, reflecting the "horse operas" favored by radio and then television audiences for decades. It is an exceedingly familiar format, and Vonnegut's success is in his ability to dismantle it point by point, yet from that dismantling to create another entirely valid work, constructed as it is with the key elements of common American aspirations. The difference is in the art behind it, once again the author's triumph in drawing on his own creative personality.

At the heart of that personality is Vonnegut's background among and within the American middle class. Combined with the inter-textuality of his *Saturday Evening Post* characters, his ho-hum familiarity with the otherwise exotic materials of outer space translates what might have been an arcane, esoteric piece of science fiction into a thoroughly comfortable style of comedy, feasting on the style of skeptical humor Americans delight in using to deflate the pretenses of glamour, riches, and brainy expertise—three aspects of space opera that are systematically deconstructed in *The Sirens of Titan*. Malachi Constant, "the richest man in America," is dragged through any number of humiliations in the process of teaching him the values of a more democratic outlook on life. Winston Niles Rumfoord, a scion of old wealth and responsibility, prevails only by emulating the unifying policies of Franklin Delano Roosevelt, the historical figure on whom he is based. Even the aliens from outer space, Vonnegut's creatures from the transgalactical planet Tralfamadore, bear a disarming familiarity: for all the world they look like that most commonly vulgar of household appliances, the plumber's helper.

These techniques of description, characterization, and theme teach Vonnegut's readers a helpful lesson in not taking the claptrap of space opera so seriously, no mean accomplishment in an age that celebrated the self-seriousness of Robert Heinlein, L. Ron Hubbard, and Arthur C. Clarke (the last of whom Vonnegut would cleverly mock in that same moon launch essay). Uncritical science fiction, like uncritical science itself, breeds a two-sided intellectual arrogance that Vonnegut seeks to undercut. On the one hand, the science fiction mentality— equipped as it is with a mentality that believes any and all problems can be solved by the miracle of science—risks engendering an attitude that the earth is just a throwaway planet, easily discardable when used up as we move on to greener fields across the universe. On the other hand, this same attitude encourages an intellectual solipsism that regards human life on earth as the absolute center of all meaning, a narrative perspective from which all other creation is to be evaluated and judged. The irony is that any "superior intelligence from outer space," a common device in such novels, is really just a projection of the author's own superiority, which in the structure of space opera becomes more earth-based than ever.

A very good way of disarming such pretensions is to have one's superior intelligences look like plumber's helpers, but Vonnegut's malicious pleasure in dismantling space opera's assumptions runs to the much greater length of having these creatures rewrite the millennial epochs of human history according to the same banality. The closest to earth the Tralfamadorians get is to Titan, the largest moon of Saturn, where a flying saucer pilot named Salo has been stranded for equipment repairs. Waiting for a spare part "the size of a can opener," he is able to keep in touch with home base by reading messages his fellow Tralfamadorians have contrived to spell out across the surface of a handy message board, in this case planet Earth:

> The reply [to his distress signal] was written on Earth in huge stones on a plain in what is now England. The ruins of the reply still stand, and are known as Stonehenge. The meaning of Stonehenge in Tralfamadorian, when viewed from above, is: *"Replacement part being rushed with all possible speed."*
>
> Stonehenge wasn't the only message old Salo had received.
>
> There had been four others, all of them written on Earth.
>
> The Great Wall of China means in Tralfamadorian, when viewed from above: *"Be patient. We haven't forgotten about you."*
>
> The meaning of the Moscow Kremlin when it was first walled was: *"You will be on your way before you know it."*
>
> The meaning of the Palace of the League of Nations in Geneva, Switzerland, is: *"Pack up your things and be ready to leave on short notice."* (pp. 271–72)

In one gesture both the relative meaning of time and the comparative significance of human endeavor are neatly skewered, but for Vonnegut the key technique is that it is done via language, for the extraterrestrials express their thoughts in the most commonly familiar, even insipid forms. As in *Player Piano,* it is the novel's narrative voice that conveys this sense, even though upon investigation it proves to be Kurt Vonnegut's own. Earlier, he has deflated the pretensions of science fiction, explaining a time warp by citing *A Child's Cyclopedia of Wonders and Things to Do,* just as in his moon launch essay years later he'd demystify NASA aura by passing over their impressively self-taken literature in favor of a quote from *The Look-It-Up Book of the Stars and Planets,* another children's book. Here language both sets the context and makes the judgment of relative value, defining the awesomely sounding *chronosynclastic infundibulum* as "Infandibulum . . . what the ancient Romans like Julius Caesar and Nero called a funnel. If you don't know what a funnel is, get Mommy to show you one" (p. 15).

Introduced to the world of mass market paperbacks via *The Sirens of Titan,* Vonnegut finds it a formally suitable replacement for his short story business, which had foundered with the gradual closing of the old family weeklies. Pulp paperbacks are generated by the same formulaic structure as fiction for the *Saturday Evening Post*; Vonnegut's previous experience with science fiction allowed him to fall into the space opera form of *Sirens* quite naturally, but as his work in this new field proceeded he would quickly adopt several other popular formats, from a double-agent spy thriller (*Mother Night*) to an apocalyptic end-of-the-world novel and a riches-in-rags romance with social theory (*Cat's Cradle* and *God Bless You, Mr. Rosewater*, conceived with the paperback market in mind, rescued at the last minute for hardcover publication, but successful only in their eventual pulp editions). Yet in none of these novels does Vonnegut adopt the formula uncritically. For each he performs a subtle modification that makes the work most characteristically his own.

Mother Night (Greenwich, Conn.: Fawcett, 1962) stands as the first example of Vonnegut actively incorporating himself as a factor in his fictive texts. Although a later edition published by Harper & Row in 1966 includes a new introduction telling the autobiographical story of the Dresden firebombing and the Polish translation (1984) includes a preface adding further details about his prisoner-of-war experiences, the original state of Vonnegut's text stands as an essential self-questioning that mirrors the novel's own theme of confused identities and schizophrenic interpretations of meaning. Although the novel itself portrays the fortunes of Howard W. Campbell, Jr. in his life as an expatriate dramatist, apparent Nazi propagandist, and actual Allied counterspy, Vonnegut takes great care to frame this fiction as an ostensibly true story. The device is a simple one: as "editor" Vonnegut signs his own name to an apparatus framing "The Confessions of Howard W. Campbell, Jr."—the interior title encountered by readers of this book. Vonnegut compounds the illusion by discussing various difficulties with the translation and makes his own judgments about where Campbell has been accurate and where not. Yet while this editor's introduction helps establish the supposed authenticity of the text, it also lets Vonnegut impose some of his personal judgments— such that lies told for artistic effect may be the most beguiling form of truth, and that Campbell's greatest crime has been against his own integrity, two factors that Vonnegut's mock introduction put into play as part of the reader's experience itself.

Within the narrative, Vonnegut takes many occasions to propound his own view of common familiarity. Although World War II is being fought we never see combat action; instead, readers are given something rarely seen—a thorough commentary on what everyday domestic life was like inside Germany during the 1933–45 period. Nor are the Nazi leaders portrayed as monsters. Rather than exploit their evil to the point of making them cartoon monsters (and hence not understandable as human beings), Vonnegut shows them in moments of utter banality such as conducting intramural office Ping-Pong tournaments. As such, they take on personal dimensions and are hence knowable in a way otherwise impossible. Some of these dimensions are comic, underscoring the novel's theme of crossed identities, as when Hitler finds himself moved by Lincoln's Gettysburg Address and Roosevelt chortles with glee over the exaggerated venom of Campbell's anti-Semitic broadcasts. Neither are things one would suspect of these larger-than-life figures, but an essential part of Vonnegut's narrative strategy is to demystify their roles so that some approximation of the truth may be known.

The same crude but insinuating familiarity pervades *Cat's Cradle* (New York: Holt, Rinehart and Winston, 1963). The scientific invention that destroys the world is not fashioned by a malevolent lunatic, but rather by a comically bumbling naïf who'd rather be tinkering with dime store turtles and novelty toys, fascinated as he is by techniques without consequence. His product, a substance named Ice-9 that raises the freezing point of water so high that the entire planet solidifies, is not used by monstrous Nazis or other inhumane enemies of humanity but rather by the penny-ante ruler of a pathetic little Caribbean island whose pretensions of power are so laughable that his eventual apocalypse can only be seen as high irony. There is a religion, Bokononism, contributing a major theme to the novel—that faith must be built on self-apparent pretense and artifice to be effective, that self-seriousness leads only to destruction—but even it deconstructs itself by such touches of banality as having its holiest psalms sung as steel-band calypso tunes.

This demystifying familiarity is carried over from *Mother Night,* as is the new novel's sense of critical textuality. The narrator of *Cat's Cradle* has begun this work by trying to write a book titled *The Day the World Ended,* thinking that his subject will be the forces that devised the atomic bomb and unleashed it on Hiroshima on August 6, 1945. Instead, his investigation generates a much larger narrative that not only encompasses the past but reaches into the present to help set the course of the future: toward the real, not metaphorical, day that ends all life on earth. By this point one sees Kurt Vonnegut developing into the writer who could produce *Slaughterhouse-Five,* an even more complex example of how writing a novel eventually entails all the elements of writing itself. There the impact will be deeply involved with aesthetic philosophy; here in *Cat's Cradle* the motive is more satiric, with the author's attitude toward his text mirroring the teachings of Bokonon, that for artifice to succeed it must always maintain its identity as arbitrary convention and never succumb to temptations of absolute truth. Bokononism does this by mocking its own seriousness; Vonnegut's novel does much the same by giving chapters such nonsensical titles as "Vice-president in Charge of Volcanoes" and "When Automobiles Had Cut-glass Vases" (the references of which are clarified in comically surprising ways) and by having these chapters be as short as just a page or two. The paragraphs are proportionately short, sometimes just one sentence in length, and the sentences can be just one word. The effect is at once childlike and conclusive, showing that things are best when kept plain and simple. As *Mother Night* had demystified Nazi Germany and thrown its textual identity into the same confusion that characterized the novel's theme, so too does *Cat's Cradle* undercut its own status as a book by literally writing itself out of human existence. The action ends, in fact, with the narrator consulting Bokonon on what to do in the face of apocalypse. Why not, the religious leader suggests, write a history of human stupidity and, using it as a pillow, freeze one's self with Ice-9 in an attitude of thumbing one's nose at God. With this benediction *Cat's Cradle* ends, the novel itself becoming that book Bokonon has suggested be written.

The novel, then, winds up as a thoroughly familiar artifact, something that the reader holds right now in his or her hands. Yet that familiarity has been established by a clever sort of defamiliarization, long a technique for seeing things freshly and clearly but here accomplished by the use of even more familiar materials. The novel's religion is based on the most common of texts, a comic book advertisement for Charles Atlas's "dynamic tension" theory of muscle building. The sayings of that religion are built on vernacular transpositions of the Bible, such as "Pay no attention to Caesar. Caesar doesn't have the slightest idea what's *really* going on" (p. 88). As for the inventor of the bomb,

Cat's Cradle portrays him as a bumbling innocent, especially in the scene quoted from the man's younger son, who recalls how his older sister ran their family:

> She used to talk about how she had three children—me, Frank, and Father. She wasn't exaggerating, either. I can remember cold mornings when Frank, Father, and I would be all in a line in the front hall, and Angela would be bundling us up, treating us all exactly the same. Only I was going to kindergarten; Frank was going to junior high; and Father was going to work on the atom bomb. (p. 23)

Here Vonnegut's language follows the same structural formula of reducing everything to a bold simplicity: as the family members line up in identical fashion for their remarkably different tasks, so too does the author's language rank them in the same syntactic form. This technique expands to form a comprehensive vision of not just the Hoenikker family (whose father invents the atomic bomb and whose children contribute to the earth's freezing with Ice-9) but of how the world works in the solemn foolery of unmaking itself. Again, the key is a simple leveling, taking a familiar action and allowing it to replicate itself with no regard to the relative consequence of its subject. When Dr. Hoenikker's fascination with dime store paraphernalia (in this case how miniature turtles retract their necks) distracts him from his work on the Manhattan Project, government officials visit Angela and ask how to get her father back on track:

> She told them to take away Father's turtles. So one night they went into his laboratory and stole the turtles and the aquarium. Father never said a word about the disappearance of the turtles. He just came to work the next day and looked for things to play with and think about, and everything there was to play with and think about had something to do with the bomb. (p. 24)

With *God Bless You, Mr. Rosewater* (New York: Holt, Rinehart and Winston, 1965), Kurt Vonnegut moves not just his technique and vision but the thematic location itself to the heart of banal familiarity, at the same time using a common narrative formula. Location is important, for it involves transposing East Coast wealth and sophistication to the grubby hell-hole known as Rosewater County, Indiana, a region challenging the imagination to realize "that land anywhere could be so deathly flat, that people anywhere could be so deathly dull" (p. 47). The formula is the prince and the pauper story, by which philanthropist Eliot Rosewater moves his Park Avenue foundation offices to a shotgun attic walk-up over a liquor store in the long-forsaken ancestral hometown back in Indiana, there to use funds otherwise earmarked for symphonies, ballets, and art museums to brighten up the lives of pathetic unfortunates who've found themselves a day late and a dollar short.

Behind it all is one of Vonnegut's most direct expressions of social philosophy, answering the question on his mind since *Player Piano*: what on earth are people *for*? But in line with his use of a common formula in a familiar location, his social theory is worked out in a thoroughly unprepossessing manner—not by references to philosophers such as Marx and Mill, but to the science fiction writing of a style he himself had satirized in *The Sirens of Titan*. Early in the novel Eliot Rosewater visits the science fiction conference at Milford, Pennsylvania—a convention of science fiction writers meeting annually under the direction of author Damon Knight—and tells the audience that they, with their hackneyed formulae and preposterous themes and characters, are in fact the only writers who truly know what's going on and sincerely care about the human predicament. Their success, he indicates, is because they understand the transformative power of the imagination—how reality is not an absolute state but is merely an anthropological description, as changeable as the terms used to define it. Money can be one such term, and to prove his point he scribbles a stack of checks and passes them out to the science fiction writers. "*There's* fantasy for you," he concludes. "And you go to the bank, tomorrow, and it will all come true. It's insane that I should be able to do such a thing, with money so important." Therefore he urges them to "think about the silly ways money gets passed around, and then think up better ways" (p. 31).

Eliot's approach is, like Vonnegut's, almost childishly simple in its directness and clarity. Yet the themes it manages to engage are the equal of anything to be found in the more weighty tomes of social philosophy. In terms of appreciating how reality is a description of how what are cultural practices are naturalized into a form of absolute law, both Rosewater's and Vonnegut's approaches reflect the insights of structuralism and even deconstruction (one should remember that Roland Barthes's most effective critiques of how arbitrary signifiers take on the authority of concrete signifieds are not his theoretical works but his familiar investigations of French popular culture published in mass market weeklies and collected as *Mythologies*). Vonnegut's own understanding of the transformative power of money comes from his family's experience in the Great Depression, where events on Wall Street changed the status of their life in Indianapolis, giving young Kurt himself a lesson in how reality is no more absolute than the terms that define it—and the stock market crash had radically changed those terms. When this orientation from Vonnegut's autobiography is combined with his vernacular approach to its expression, *God Bless You, Mr. Rosewater* takes shape as his most frank (and almost overwhelmingly cynical) book.

There is no sentimentality about either Vonnegut's or Rosewater's project. The author has no illusions about how writing novels can change the world, for a practical application is needed before creative imagination can have any effect. "You can safely ignore the arts and sciences," Eliot advises. "They never helped anybody. Be a sincere, attentive friend of the poor" (p. 21). For his part the author salts his character's idealism by making the poor he serves a decidedly repulsive group; as for the results of Eliot's charity, we're shown just a few threatened suicides bargained back to life at bottom-dollar prices, plus a village oddball or two humored in his or her eccentricity. His toils take place in a hopeless, devastated landscape of strip-mined countryside and automated factories from whence the original Rosewater fortune derives. Eliot's attempt to revitalize the land by returning some of its wealth is seen as pathetic, just as the literary form Vonnegut acknowledges as the vehicle for his larger social theory is the equally unpromising one of schlock science fiction. Yet here too Vonnegut is turning to his autobiography, for the character he creates to expound these ideas—Kilgore Trout—is fashioned on his own worse fears of what the author of *Player Piano* (shabbily paperbacked as *Utopia-14*) and *The Sirens of Titan* (with its luridly suggestive cover) might become. As such, it serves as another example of Vonnegut's text undercutting itself, reminding the reader that rather than being the seat of ultimate authority the book is just one more artifact, as arbitrary and imperfect as anything fashioned by a man or a woman can be.

Readers, not authors, are the vehicle of change, this approach implies, for in addition to all his personal unsavoriness Kilgore Trout must admit that all his books are out of print. Eliot Rosewater, however, has read them when they were available and has fashioned his life according to those fictional ideals. Trout's message is a very simple one: that the older American ethic, by which people have been valued according to the work they do and value they produce, can no longer be valid in a world of automation where the need for such work has been removed. People must be valued simply for what they *are,* Trout teaches—to be loved uncritically, in other words. The genius of this novel is not in having Trout say these things but seeing Eliot Rosewater put them into practice. His motto is equally simple but more charmingly effective in its practice: "Pretend to be good always, and even God will be fooled" (p. 203). His disarming candor is part of the new mythology Trout says is needed to replace the outworn American dream of boundless opportunity predicated on hard work. One such form of mythology is Eliot's baptism service, the words of which are as simple and direct as his philanthropic approach: "Hello, babies. Welcome to Earth. It's hot in the summer and cold in the winter. It's round and wet and crowded. At the outside, babies, you've got about a hundred years here. There's only one rule that I know of, babies—: 'God damn it, you've got to be kind' " (p. 110). From a simple welcome to the most obvious facts of annual life, Rosewater's statement establishes a level of familiarity that only gently moves into interpretive sociology (the world being "crowded"). With their maximum of a century on the planet, the existence of just one rule does not seem overly minimal, especially when its dictum is so universally embracing. Yet the entire statement is formulated with no more complexity than its simple additive syntax. It's the voice of a convinced reader who has been exposed to new ideas and is now expressing them not as an author, science fiction or otherwise, but as a common human being. It is the stance Kurt Vonnegut himself has chosen to take, discounting his own posture as a writer of books in the process, speaking conversationally at all times and letting his textual devices undercut themselves.

Such undercutting reaches its technical climax in *Slaughterhouse-Five* (New York: Delacorte Press/Seymour Lawrence, 1969), in which Vonnegut makes the greatest use of himself as a self-present author involved in writing this novel even as its narrative devices function to cancel each other out. His general approach is the same as for his previous novels: taking the most extraordinary particulars and confronting them with a skeptical, hands-in-his-pockets attitude that reveals them as sharing the most humble and familiar of American middle-class experiences. As always, his strategy is to take whatever startling new developments his changing culture offers up and make sense of them by drawing a relation with something in his own life's story, but the great technical advance of *Slaughterhouse-Five* is that here Vonnegut makes this autobiographical relationship a matter of structure as well as theme.

The essence of Vonnegut's story consists in confessing how difficult it has been to write it. Such commentary might exist traditionally outside the text of a novel, and if he had other intentions in mind Vonnegut might well have designated his opening and closing chapters as the book's preface and afterward. But his struggles with the formal materials of *Slaughterhouse-Five* are central to the novel's real subject, and so his commentary on how hard it has been for him to even remember his adventures in the war, much less write them down, is titled "Chapter One," while his summation of the action's close and his own finishing up of the job of writing comes in as "Chapter Ten," with no segmentation from the otherwise fictive narrative at all.

Vonnegut's professed struggles in writing this novel are much more than a simple foregrounding of technique and authorial presence, which are, after all, techniques as old as the genre itself. Instead, they are the way he places his own autobiography into the story. In previous novels these personal references had been thematic—veiled references to General Electric, value systems spawned by his Midwestern youth, the behavior patterns of Americans in middle-class contexts such as his own—but in *Slaughterhouse-Five* they become structural, for Vonnegut's presence in the narrative is not simply as a native of Indianapolis or a former worker for General Electric but as the novel's author, working away even as his book takes shape. Yet this authorial insertion serves the same purpose as references to the experiences and values of his autobiography had in previous works: it keeps the narrative direct, honest, and unassuming, protecting it from unwarranted but easily made assumptions which cloud the truth.

In *Player Piano* those false assumptions had been about the presumed values of automation; in *The Sirens of Titan* they'd been previously unquestioned ideals of free will and relative importance within the cosmic scheme of things. In similar ways *Mother Night* had demystified life within Nazi Germany, *Cat's Cradle* had robbed apocalypse of its truth-effacing fire, and *God Bless You, Mr. Rosewater* had thrown off balance the most mythological of American values. In

Slaughterhouse-Five, however, the enemies of plain truth and clear thinking are technical devices concerned with how stories are told, particularly in the case of war stories, the forms of which tend to falsify the true nature of experience. This is the problem Vonnegut struggles with in Chapter One. He tells about returning from the war believing that writing a book about his unique act of witness at Dresden will make him rich and famous; instead, he finds that all details of the firebombing are top secret and that even those he wishes to tell about the event are more interested in countering his story with their extensive claims about the Holocaust. As the years go by, he finds that his own memory has been effaced in the process, and so he turns to what should be a credible authority, his POW colleague Bernard O'Hare. What he learns on this visit, however, is not something about the authority of authorship but rather a lesson from the audience for such stories, O'Hare's wife Mary, who faults such tales for glorifying wars which were in truth nothing but pathetic children's crusades.

Therefore, keeping his pledge to Mary O'Hare that his novel won't fall into the old stereotypes of glorified war stories, Vonnegut keeps himself inside his book as a way of preventing traditional styles and structures from intruding on the innovative material he wishes to present. Its essence is that it is unspeakable; in trying to speak about such atrocities, previous novels have filled what should be an essential void with all sorts of false feeling and false writing. In his initial thoughts about drafting such a story Vonnegut confesses to imagining heroic roles for himself and his colleagues, transforming himself and them into John Waynes and Frank Sinatras, for these had been the transpositions he'd witnessed in previous war narratives. As a testimony to his own integrity as a writer, however, his novel refuses to let itself be written this way. In time the act of struggle becomes its substance, but even here the strategy is more than just a metafictional play with self-reflection. Because of the special approach he takes to his material, Kurt Vonnegut manages to remain both inside and outside of his narrative, interacting with the characters he has created yet still standing above them—not so much in juxtaposition to them as their maker but in relation to the readers as the author of the tale they're reading. As such, he manages to control all three aspects of the fictive act: writing, reading, and the performative narrative action by which writer and reader meet. In Chapter One Vonnegut summarizes his Dresden experience and tells how hard it has been to write about it.

In Chapter Ten he concludes both his fictive action and his own act of writing it, eventually uniting the two acts by lamenting the death of Robert Kennedy (which has occurred during the writing of these last pages) and then returning to the bombing's aftermath in Dresden, where he himself (as a historical personage, on the order of Robert Kennedy) joins Billy Pilgrim and the other characters as corpse miners. Within the novel's eight middle chapters, he has also appeared three times on the action's periphery—sick in a latrine, watching a captured American colonel trying to find his troops, and remarking that the as yet unbombed city of Dresden looks like the land of Oz. Thus he creates a multidimensional narrative with three focuses: the person who actually experienced these events in history, the person who has struggled to write about them for over twenty years until finding a way to create the narrative of Billy Pilgrim, and ultimately the person who now finally completes the book, a work joining the history of human achievement that now, as its final typescript page has been completed, also includes the fresh news that Robert Kennedy has died.

Vonnegut has a comment on the Kennedy assassination—"so it goes"—which is repeated ninety-nine other times in the narrative, a formulation used whenever something animated dies, be it a person, animal, or bubbles in champagne. This repetition has the same multi-dimensional effect as Vonnegut's own layering of experiential and compositional history and therefore accomplishes the same leveling: a person witnesses a massacre and a person writes a book of fiction, each act having its own historical reality and deserving to be judged not as inspirations for or representations of the other, but as validly existing things in themselves. In a similar way no death is any more or less important than any other, at least in the ultimate scheme of things; to keep matters in proportion, one must remember that death is so common and inevitable that one cannot lose the ability to exist in the face of it, even as sentiment would tempt. Thus the strategy for structuring *Slaughterhouse-Five* complements its theme, both of which are radical innovations within the traditional ways of writing about and responding to wartime death.

As the first of Vonnegut's innovatively personal novels (following his subgeneric adaptations from *Player Piano* through *God Bless You, Mr. Rosewater*), *Slaughterhouse-Five* displays the wealth of narrative material that can be generated by this new relationship between the world of the actual and that of the mind creating another world by means of imaginative interaction with it. The true action of the novel proceeds toward a kind of peace between author and subject, a silence which commemorates the unspeakable nature of the Dresden massacre. Chapter One has dealt with the obstacles Kurt Vonnegut himself encountered in trying to put his experiences on paper, but throughout the succeeding chapters his characters are confronted by various formulaic responses to war which must be dismissed because of their fraudulence. The British prisoners-of-war, for example, have styled themselves as models from a romantic past: "They were adored by the Germans, who thought they were exactly what Englishmen ought to be. They made war look stylish and reasonable and fun" (p. 81). The truth of their comfortable survival, however, is based on a series of lies: their bonhomie, shared with the Americans, does not extend to the Russian prisoners, who strike them as Slavic, dull, and of no help to them; their perception of the American prisoners is based on a mythology that bitter reality soon discounts; and the very nature of their well-being is thanks to a clerical mistake which has been sending them five hundred Red Cross parcels each month instead of the intended and proper fifty. But the British are not the only ones driven by a mystique. The American infantryman Roland Weary tries to fabricate a "Three Musketeers" spirit among himself and two unwilling scouts; his colleague Paul Lazzaro believes everything can be solved by mob-style vengeance; the more sympathetically attractive Edgar Derby preaches and practices a gospel of kindness and courtesy, but is executed by Germans, amid the mass annihilation and catastrophic destruction of Dresden, for the innocuous act of picking up a tea pot. These specific forms of reaction to the war are joined by larger national interpretations, including the Americans' undisciplined selfishness and the Nazis' propaganda line as announced by the protagonist borrowed from *Mother Night,* Howard Campbell. Like the glamorous war movies criticized by Mary O'Hare in Chapter One, these responses have to be overcome as well before the essential truth within Vonnegut's narrative can be found.

In this process the reader is replicating Vonnegut's own search for valid expression. There is a strong temptation to admire the initially attractive portraits of the British POWs and of Edgar Derby, just as Kurt Vonnegut admits his first intentions to write a narrative in the mode of a 1940s bestseller. As authors are conditioned by their cultures to write a certain way, so too are readers prompted to read in accepted manners—admiring individually strong examples of self-discipline and generosity toward others. Such specific examples, however, are not the issue; being conditioned to respond a certain way is, and it is this involuntary response that prevents both the makers and readers of narratives from getting at the truth of such inevitable and perennial catastrophes as unjust acts of war.

To break this conditioning process Vonnegut scrambles almost every recognizable convention of the traditional novel. His own overt presence as its writer in Chapters One and Ten is the initial shock, but it is quickly followed by the radical antichronology his narrative assumes in chapter two and sustains nearly to the end. As a technical device, this simultaneity of time frames is called "time travel," as in a science fiction manner his protagonist Billy Pilgrim is shuttled from moment to moment among radically diverse places and eras. But in terms of the reader's response, these shifts can be characterized as mental wanderings, imaginative transpositions, or associations based on spatial rather than temporal links. Either way, the method effectively disrupts a conventional reading, especially one that seeks to acquire a logically accumulating meaning. Instead, the reader is forced to appreciate each scene for itself and not draw any conclusion about it until the end, when the entire collage of such moments comes together and the novel itself takes shape all at once. In addition, Vonnegut uses other means of structuring his narrative according to something other than linear causality. There are haunting verbal repetitions, a distillation of recurring images, and significant identifications that pull the narrative sequences together in a virtually subliminal way. Russian prisoners surrounding the British POW camp have pale faces looking like "radium dials" (p. 78); just one page before the same description is supplied for the face of a watch glowing in the darkness of Carlsbad Caverns. The train transporting Billy Pilgrim to Dresden is painted with orange and black stripes, just as is the caterer's tent at the party for his wedding anniversary. And of course there are the one hundred incantations of the phrase "so it goes," as unifying a motif as is death itself.

Complementing this subtle coherency is Vonnegut's increasing use of intertextuality—which, like the structural imposition of his own autobiographical values and experiences, is a very personal affair. *Slaughterhouse-Five* draws a set of locations and a cast of supporting characters from all of his previous novels. Billy Pilgrim's hometown is

Ilium, New York, the location for *Player Piano* and much of *Cat's Cradle*; he spends his postwar years there as an optometrist selling safety glasses to the workers at General Forge and Foundry, the giant corporation whose research lab employed Dr. Felix Hoenikker and whose plant will be fully automated in the future of Vonnegut's dystopian novel. The Nazi Germany where Billy is held as a prisoner of war is a locale first used in *Mother Night*; drawn from that work is Howard Campbell, making a guest appearance in Vonnegut's new novel. *The Sirens of Titan* supplies the outer space aliens known as Tralfamadorians, while *God Bless You, Mr. Rosewater* has previously introduced the science fiction author who writes about them, Kilgore Trout. Billy's family life has elements taken from the pages of *Collier's* and *The Saturday Evening Post,* where Vonnegut's short stories had been appearing from 1950 through 1962, years paralleling his protagonist's domestic adventures. Even if the readers of *Slaughterhouse-Five* did not recognize all these borrowings, their presence made the book something thoroughly familiar to Vonnegut himself, who was now drawing on experiences he himself had created and not merely lived.

Kilgore Trout is one such creation the author keeps employed for some time, and the different ways in which he is used indicate Vonnegut's transition from subgeneric formulas to increasingly personal structures, a move paralleling his own change in status from a neglected and virtually unknown writer to one of the country's most famous public spokesmen. In *God Bless You, Mr. Rosewater* Trout appears only near the end, when Eliot's ideals need a spokesman; in terms of textuality his presence is a device whereby Vonnegut can incorporate his ideas directly, rather than simply showing Eliot as having responded to them. In *Slaughterhouse-Five* Trout's personal appearance again comes near the end, but his stories and novels are referred to throughout, creating a true sense of intertextuality by which the effect of Vonnegut's own narrative is multiplied several fold. Rather than actually writing all of these works (and Trout is staggeringly prolific), Vonnegut simply refers to their themes and statements as if they have been written, a technique appreciated by a writer no less sophisticated and innovative than Jorge Luis Borges, whose "imaginary library" contained just such countless resources. His next novel, however, uses Trout even more creatively, involving him directly with the novel's action throughout; when someone makes a late appearance to expound ideas and pull strings, it is not Trout but Kurt Vonnegut himself.

Breakfast of Champions (New York: Delacorte Press/Seymour Lawrence, 1973) is structured by a crisscross pattern involving the two poles of literary experience: that of a writer, Kilgore Trout, making his way to a cultural festival in his honor, and Dwayne Hoover, a reader of one of Trout's fictions that explains the distressing nature of existence in shockingly simple terms: the great mad world is just an illusion, being projected by a solitary existing reader now clued into the truth by God. Hoover makes the fundamental error that Trout teases a naive party-goer about in *Slaughterhouse-Five*: that whatever is published is the truth. Devastated by this information, the hapless reader attempts suicide and lives out the rest of his life insane. Trout himself is pictured as a pathetically ineffectual old man, the image of Vonnegut's father in his sadly declining years, which prompts the author to enter his own story, manipulate the narrative action, and personally set his creation free.

Kurt Vonnegut's personal involvement with his fiction is now complete, for it involves not just homegrown characters, scenes, and values (such as constituted his first five novels), nor just his talking about his own work in writing the book (as happens in *Slaughterhouse-Five*), but—in addition to all of these features—his active presence within the text itself, not as a participating character (such as his three cameo appearances along the road to Dresden and in the holocaust's aftermath) but as the personally responsible and responsive creator of all that happens—as the God, in other words, who has driven Dwayne Hoover insane. Similar responsibility haunted Mark Twain in the last decade of his life, and texts like the successive drafts of *The Mysterious Stranger* show him struggling to come to terms with its energy. For Vonnegut, thankfully, this realization has come in mid-career rather than near its end, and in this and subsequent novels he begins with an extensive autobiographical preface, locating himself in relation to the text. The first such enfolding had been in 1966, with the new introduction written to the Harper & Row hardcover of *Mother Night*, and for the next two decades Vonnegut maintains the practice as an integral part of each fictive work, from the strongly self-analytical (even self-critical) preface to *Welcome to the Monkey House* to the extended (and personally revealing) dedication to *Galápagos*. In each case his responsibility for the subsequent narrative is acknowledged, its existence justified by being traced to a key part of the author's autobiography. Part of Mark Twain's dilemma was that the doings of his fiction struck him as arbitrary and gratuitous; if the story were to entail suffering, he felt personally responsible for it, as culpable as a heartless God punishing his creatures at whim. By means of his prefaces, all of which are analytical, confessional, and self-probing affairs, Vonnegut justifies his actions in proceeding with his narrative—to the reader, of course, but most of all to himself.

The things discussed by Vonnegut in his preface to *Breakfast of Champions* prepare the way for both the novel's thematics and structure, particularly for how its themes structure the void of an otherwise graspable content. Just as the initial chapter of *Slaughterhouse-Five* asked a question—"What do you say about a massacre?"—and implied that its answer would consist in avoiding the many false solutions traditional war narratives offer, so does *Breakfast of Champions'* preface trace its way along "a sidewalk strewn with junk, trash which I throw over my shoulder as I travel back in time to November eleventh, nineteen hundred and twenty-two" (p. 6)—fifty years back to the author's birthday, then celebrated in reverence as Armistice Day in commemoration of another event of absolute quiet, the moment when the guns of the Great War fell silent. Old battlefield veterans have told him it was as if "the sudden silence was the Voice of God" (p. 6). Like Twain's God responsible for his own creations, Vonnegut strives to discard all impediments to capturing that silence in his work, only to have its final words turn back to him. Not in blame for responsibility, or as an indictment for writing, but rather as an insight into the autobiographical genesis of his fictive work.

Writing a full novel about Kilgore Trout, who in two previous novels has been just the author's device for articulating his own beliefs, allows Vonnegut to face his own condition as a writer, to explore his work's strategy and effects, to gain distance from and therefore draw perspective on its meaning, and to examine his own deepest fear, that "I have no culture, no humane harmony in my brains. I can't live without a culture anymore" (p. 5). As a step beyond the willful silence of *Slaughterhouse-Five,* this new novel serves as the attempt of an innovative, even experimental author to recover, in a posthumanistic world, a revalidated sense of humanity.

Part of his method is to deconstruct the previous mode of what passed for humane behavior, starting with the hallowed principles on which the United States of America is founded. Like a poststructuralist critic, Vonnegut takes the most familiar texts and reveals how their meanings are not at all inherent but have rather been naturalized by long cultural use, their supposed truths being nothing other than consensus assumptions. Close reading makes for a good start, such as laboring through the familiar verses of "O Say Can You See?" so slowly and self-consciously that its apparency finally dawns on the reader: of all the "quadrillion nations in the Universe" the United States "was the only one with a national anthem which was gibberish sprinkled with question marks" (p. 8). Vonnegut's deliberately empirical, doggedly simplistic recitation of American history, stripped clean of its enhancing mythology, yields the same result:

> Actually, the sea pirates who had the most to do with the creation of the new government owned human slaves. They used human beings for machinery, and, even after slavery was eliminated, continued to think of ordinary human beings as machines.
>
> The sea pirates were white. The people who were already on the continent when the pirates arrived were copper-colored. When slavery was introduced onto the continent, the slaves were black.
>
> Color was everything. (p. 11)

To emphasize the harsh clarity of this new perspective, Vonnegut pauses every few pages to illustrate a point in the most naked and obvious way, with a simple felt-pen drawing. The result is much like the regular repetition of "so it goes" on the occasion of each death in his preceding novel, reminding readers of the simple essence of a thing and also of its inexorability. *There it is,* says the text, in a manner detached from the relativity of language and shown so plainly that we are forced to see what rhetoric and myth obscure.

As *Breakfast of Champions* takes on this general quality of deconstructing what one may have assumed to be obvious, so do Kilgore Trout's summarized fictions exploit the irony of transposed perspective: "Kilgore Trout once wrote a short story which was a dialogue between two pieces of yeast. They were discussing the possible purposes of life as they ate sugar and suffocated in their own excrement. Because of their limited intelligence, they never came close to guessing that they were making champagne" (pp. 208–9). Trout's perspective on human life is equally bleak: people are just factors in a cruel routine of "destructive testing," being pitted against the hopeless odds of a mechanical world to see how much punishment they can bear. But balancing this view is the interpretation voiced by a creative artist, the abstract expressionist painter Rabo Karabekian (who will be developed later as the protagonist of *Bluebeard*). As minimally effective as they are, all living things are characterized by their self-awareness, the quality that makes them animate. Karabekian's painting portrays the band of light evoking the presence of such self-awareness; simply because it is *there,* it demands attention and even reverence, a quality highlighted in the strongly spiritual painters on whose work Karabekian's is modeled, Barnett Newman and Mark Rothko. "Our awareness is all that is alive and maybe sacred in any of us," he teaches. "Everything else about us is dead machinery" (p. 221). The theory complements Trout's and redeems it, offering the chance for uncritical love the science fiction writer himself had called for two novels earlier.

In *Breakfast of Champions* Vonnegut conducts a running argument with the illusory traditions of realistic fiction, arguing that the same self-apparency that's obvious in Karabekian's work is needed for novels to do their job. Imposing an order where none is possible creates false expectations; mechanical devices for ending the patently indivisible flow of life, such as conveniently conclusive murders, simply encourage imitation by people wanting their own experiences to have such facile markers. To remind both himself and his readers that everything in *Breakfast of Champions* is completely fabricated, Vonnegut joins its progress before the conclusion, walking into scenes and pulling funny little tricks like making a phone ring to distract one character so that he can concentrate on another. Once inside his story he is faced with the creative nature of his own work, learning the deeper nature of responsibility that so tragically eluded Mark Twain. Wishing to release the pathetic, enfeebled Kilgore Trout from further narrative service, he finds his character taking the previously unrecognized shape of his inspiration: Vonnegut's own father near the end of his life. And what this inspiration requests of him is something only totally self-apparent art can achieve—to make this old man young again. As an everyday equivalent to the predicament faced when asked to say something about a massacre in *Slaughterhouse-Five,* Vonnegut had shown Billy Pilgrim facing his aged mother's question, "How did I get so old?" *Breakfast of Champions* finds the author himself hearing a similar request, but this time around he has moved inside the narrative himself, where—with the ideological and aesthetic doctrines of Kilgore Trout and Rabo Karabekian in hand—he stands a chance of finding a workable answer. Popular science fiction and abstract expressionist painting are two of America's most original contributions to the world of artistic creation, and from their familiarity Vonnegut draws continued strength for his own fiction.

At the beginning of *Breakfast of Champions* Vonnegut makes a significant move toward defining the practicality of the arts, something his earlier character Eliot Rosewater had despaired of. The occasion is the awarding of the Nobel Prize to Kilgore Trout: not in literature, for the art of his fiction, but in medicine, for his proof that ideas have medicinal and physiological effects. In *Slapstick* (Delacorte Press/Seymour Lawrence, 1976) the author makes another statement about ideas: that they have no meaningful content, but are simply functional as badges of friendship, thereby earning their importance as sociological rather than simply conceptual elements. From them the relative health or sickness of an entire society will be derived. The basic idea that generates the plot of *Slapstick* is characteristically Vonnegutian in its familiarity, simplicity, and directness. The protagonist, Wilbur Swain, campaigns successfully for the presidency by proposing that every citizen will be given a new middle name, making him or her a member in an artificially extended family that will take on responsibility for the care of its own. The novel's structure is announced in its autobiographical prologue, which, like the technically similar preface to *Breakfast of Champions,* presents the terms by which the author will organize his work. For *Slapstick* the key principles are remembering the death of Vonnegut's beloved sister (which he sees as an exceptionally wicked punishment by fate—she died of cancer just a few days after her husband perished in an absurdly improbable train wreck, orphaning four children) but also recalling how the great slapstick comedians of the American 1930s endured similarly maddening accidents yet managed to look funny in the process (and thereby bringing laughter and relief to their beleaguered countrymen suffering through the Great Depression). In terms of his autobiography Vonnegut can see the structural approach these topics provide: crude and cruel slapstick humor is indeed what life seems like to him, with its endless tests of his limited intelligence and agility, yet the fundamental joke of the great slapstick comedians (such as Laurel & Hardy) was that "they did their best with every test. They never failed to bargain in good faith with their destinies, and were screamingly adorable and funny on that account" (p. 1). Their comic reaction is the one Vonnegut adopts to make his own account of the trials of life proportionately adorable and funny—just the opposite of Dwayne Hoover's response in the previous novel and therefore one that is more hopeful and attractive.

The joke structure itself is one especially attractive to Vonnegut. In his public speaking he is fond of both using it and explaining how it works. He will ask his audience a question—what is the speed of light, the capital of Peru, the dates of Napoleon Bonaparte's lifetime—and almost immediately hit them with another, such as "Why is the price of cream so high?" He gives them a moment to ponder, and then supplies the answer: "Because the cows really hate squatting over those tiny bottles." His response is guaranteed to generate a laugh, unexceptional as the joke is, for a very specific reason which Vonnegut is pleased to explain. When people are asked a question, he argues, they are forced to do some hard mental work, plus fear not knowing the correct answer. And so when he quickly tells them the comic response to his second question, his audience is relieved—relieved because they no longer have to work at something, because they are no longer under the pressure of coming up with a correct answer. Two principles are at work here: tension and relief. Tension is set by the mechanics of the initially serious question and the second uncertain one; it is relieved when the tension is sprung, the patent silliness of cows squatting over little cream bottles revealing that his listeners haven't been put on the spot at all. It is as simple as setting and springing a mousetrap, Vonnegut explains; but because one joke structure must be set and sprung before the next one can be rigged, his narratives must proceed a page at a time, each little bit of slapstick humor engineered to perfection.

With its narrator-protagonist as the president of the United States, *Slapstick* signals another transition in Vonnegut's writing career that also parallels his life. From now on his central characters will be publicly famous like himself, with their thematic and structural involvements resulting from the special nature of their notoriety. On the heels of the Watergate scandal Vonnegut creates a narrator marginally involved in it, Walter Starbuck, whose fate is to end a career of idealistic government service as an unwitting accomplice of Richard Nixon's malefactors. *Jailbird* (Delacorte Press/Seymour Lawrence, 1979) serves as his attempt to be reborn into the world after his imprisonment for the Nixon administration's crime, just as several of the real president's men confessed to being reborn to a new sense of spirituality during their years in jail. But in this case "rebirth" means a creatively imaginative act, signaled by the presence of Kilgore Trout— not freed from further service, as Vonnegut had promised him at the end of *Breakfast of Champions,* but made young again as he had requested. In this new novel Trout is more than ever a textual factor; his identity itself is as a pen name for a fellow prison inmate, Robert Fender, whose naive romanticism has allowed him to blunder into an act of unintended treason twenty years before. The fictions of "Kilgore Trout," then, have been written from prison, vain attempts to reinvent a world in which the writer can no longer live.

As for the novel's protagonist, Walter Starbuck, he follows Robert Fender's example of reimagining a world with all of its previously distracting clutter stripped bare—a vision possible for one whose lifelong career has been discredited and who now reemerges from prison unfettered by obligations to either failure or success. His newly clarified vision allows Vonnegut to make points in his most comfort- able way, revealing what the truth of life can be, if only we let ourselves see them for what they are. Stripped of all sophistications and reduced to bare essentials, Starbuck wanders around New York City, lost and lonely until he finds himself lingering before the suddenly awesome spectacle of a coffee shop working full tilt for the morning rush. He's intimidated by all the action:

> But I somehow found the courage to go in anyway—and imagine my surprise! It was as though I had died and gone to heaven! A waitress said to me, "Honeybunch, you sit right down, and I'll bring you your coffee right away." I hadn't said anything to her.
>
> So I did sit down, and everywhere I looked I saw customers of every description being received with love. To the waitresses everybody was "honeybunch" and "dear." It was like an emer- gency ward after a great catastrophe. It did not matter what race or class the victims belonged to. They were all given the same miracle drug, which was coffee. The catastrophe in this case, of course, was that the sun had come up again. (p. 123)

Note how both the problem and its solution are reduced to elements so basic as to efface their previously threatening nature. And consider how simple the structuring method is. If there is a void at the center of things, Vonnegut makes it a comfortable one, reminding us that it has been the needlessly complicated desire to fill that void with distracting content that has created a troublesome life in the first place. In his prologue Vonnegut has cited a high school student's appraisal of his works' meaning: "Love may fail, but courtesy will prevail" (p. x). *Jailbird* demonstrates this truth in its protagonist's actions, most of which consist of discovering how Kilgore Trout's earlier prescription for uncritical love can be fulfilled. At first appearing like a shallow sentiment, this dictum is carried out by systematically deconstructing the fraudulent and ineffective devices used to fill the void of subject, revealing in the end that process rather than product—an act as simple as a sunrise coffee shop service—is the most helpfully corrective solution.

Using this process as a guide, *Jailbird* turns to reinventing the American dream. The mass of property that *God Bless You, Mr. Rosewater* had found so ill-distributed is now redistributed by gathering it all together and then breaking it into an infinite number of parts deeded back to the country's citizens. The failed student romance of Walter Starbuck and Mary O'Looney is recovered and reshaped according to the simpler and more achievable goal of common decency. Christianity can be cruel, especially when left to the devices of those who would use it to absolutize their own relative beliefs; Vonnegut's novel reinterprets its teachings with an eye toward making an allowance for Christ's "slightly crazy" days (p. 38). Most important of all, kindness is rewarded in a way that the American economic system can handle. Profit motives by themselves are destructive, but simple rituals based on mutual respect can keep life moving in nondestructive ways. As for the manner in which Kurt Vonnegut the writer accomplishes this, one of *Jailbird*'s closing scenes offers a good analogy. Mary O'Looney is dying, and the ambulance attendants taking her away are Pakistanis who converse in Urdu, a language that fascinates Walter Starbuck:

> I inquired of them, in order to calm the sobs that were welling up inside of me, to tell me a little about Urdu. They said it had a literature as great as any in the world, but that it had begun as a spare and ugly artificial language invented in the court of Ghengis Khan. Its purpose in the beginning was military. It allowed his captains to give orders that were understood in every part of the Mongol Empire. Poets would later make it beautiful. (p. 222)

This novel is a parallel attempt to transform the economic system of America, its original dream, into something less personally offensive, thanks to the language of poetry and kindness.

As *Jailbird* evaluates and restructures the American economic dream, Vonnegut's next novel considers the role of the arts in our culture. As is now customary, the author begins with an autobiographical preface explaining his personal relation to the narrative's images and symbols; primary among them is the relationship between the story's empty, unappreciated arts center and his own seat of artistic genius—and so both broadly cultural and specifically personal aesthetic issues are to be jointly examined. This interplay characterizes the form of *Deadeye Dick* (New York: Delacorte Press/Seymour Lawrence, 1982), in which the fortunes of Rudy Waltz are plotted against the larger cultural and artistic interests of his family and community.

In terms of both culture and art, there is a strong Eurocentric interest that determines the course of Rudy's father's life. A self-confessed dilettante, he masquerades through the decline of European art as a way of counterfeiting an aesthetic reputation—his play at being a painter is an excuse for fancy living, a style he brings back to America and in which he raises his son. Their family life is a mélange of obsolescent claptrap, with Rudy being born in an antique bed brought home from Vienna over which hangs a painting by a young Austrian met during student days abroad, Adolf Hitler. But the evil in Rudy's life comes from another part of his father's European collection, an assemblage of firearms comprising almost the entire history of such weaponry. It is Rudy's careless misuse of one of these rifles that gives him his nickname, Deadeye Dick, for in surrendering to his whim to fire the rifle aimlessly across the city he inadvertently kills a pregnant young mother miles away. Combined with the geopolitical actions of his father's friend Hitler, Rudy's European legacy proves to be dire indeed.

The central action of *Deadeye Dick* is not the unintended manslaughter, however, but rather concerns Rudy's inability to grow up and lead a life independent of his parents' phony culture and the definitions their irresponsibilities have placed upon him. In a way his desire to flee the world's ugliness by living within an escapist retreat mirrors his father's lust for the flippant trivialities of a once great European culture in decline. "Dead storage" is the term Vonnegut's narrative uses for each; only as the novel progresses does Rudy learn that he must emerge from this lifeless refuge, take control of the elements of his life, and recreate himself by means of art. Granted, those elements themselves may add up to a big nothing—indeed, his hometown of Midland City is described as a nothing writ large, and therefore suitable as the testing ground for America's first neutron bomb. But it is in the act of structuring that void that Rudy creates an identity; by doing so he is independent of his parents and their culture for the first time and thereby is not Deadeye Dick anymore. In the process his traumatic experiences can be transformed into self-knowledge and self-responsibility that heal. As his own creator, he writes from a hotel in Haiti—the same hotel from which Vonnegut signs his preface. The correlation between author and subject is thus made in terms of Rudy telling his story and Vonnegut writing his book.

Emphasizing the textuality of this approach are two items Rudy Waltz inserts routinely into his narrative: small "playlets" in which he takes control of an embarrassing event by ordering it as a drama (and hence redeeming his own part) and recipes for various meals either being eaten by his characters at the time or thematically related to their actions. Each technique reminds the reader that there is a narrative concoction taking place and that Rudy is the one doing the concocting—a necessary reminder, since so much of *Deadeye Dick*'s action involves his humiliation. Yet even as these practices emphasize the novel's void of appreciable subject matter, its breadth of action is filled with the narrator's self-apparent structurings, which like all of Vonnegut's textual devices are simple and unassuming, as familiar as anything the readers themselves may have done (filing a favorite recipe, rehearsing an imaginative fantasy as a way of redeeming one's behavior).

In *Deadeye Dick* these textual insertions punctuate the narrative, standing out by virtue of their exceptional form. For *Galápagos* (Delacorte Press/Seymour Lawrence, 1985) Vonnegut goes a step farther by casting his narrative all in one piece, yet referring constantly to various epochs in time over a million year range. As in his previous novel, the narrator holds the key. Here he is Leon Trout, son of the science fiction writer, who (following service in and desertion from the Vietnam War) has been killed in an industrial accident during the construction of the ship on which much of the novel's action will take place. Because Leon has declined to enter the afterlife (a technique adopted from his father's science fiction mythology), he remains as a ghost to follow the novel's action, which begins with a near apocalypse (destroying all but the passengers on board for a nature cruise to Darwin's famous Galápagos Islands) and ranges on to a perspectival present of a million years past 1986 A.D. Again, the ostensible subject matter of Leon's narrative is so simple as to hardly bear explaining: over the course of these million years, human beings have re-evolved into a species far less dangerous to themselves and to nature, their too-large brains shrinking to a much smaller capacity and their mischievous hands and fingers reforming as swim flippers. What makes the narrative remarkable is Leon's structuring of the event, and that structuring is facilitated by the many periods of time he is able to collapse into one constantly present view. Whatever detestable actions take place over this course of time he can relate, in anthropological fashion, to the corrupt nature of the war he himself fought (for this volume Vonnegut describes himself as a trained anthropologist with a graduate degree from the University of Chicago). But in addition to lessons from history and anthropology, Leon can also draw comparisons to his own family life, where his mother's warm sympathy contrasts with his father's bitterly sardonic vision. That vision itself has been expressed in putative texts that Leon can quote, just as Vonnegut himself was able to do in *God Bless You, Mr. Rosewater, Slaughterhouse-Five, Breakfast of Champions,* and *Jailbird.* As the action progresses, Leon is able to make comparisons with his personal experience and the legacy of his times, both of which contribute to the possibilities of nuclear annihilation. However, his narrative stance allows these judgments to be made across the breadth of an additional million years of human history, its facets multiplying in proportion to the references Leon is able to make to conditions circa 1986. As a result, the novel expands far beyond its hard-core subject, to engage questions that are political, sociological, anthropological, and even theological. That expansion is due simply to Leon Trout's ability to structurally multiply the smallest factor. As such, *Galápagos* is Vonnegut's most exponentially powerful novel.

It is not surprising, then, that his next work, *Bluebeard* (New York: Delacorte Press, 1987), would use this same structural principle. In *Slaughterhouse-Five* multiple periods of time had been referenced by means of a mechanical science fiction device: time travel. To justify that technique the author had invented an entire race of extraterrestrials with their own coherent philosophy and physics of time. Even *Galápagos* draws on similar structural stylistics, the afterlife being a blue tunnel into which one's ancestors beckon; only the fact that Leon Trout resists his science-fiction-writer father's invitation allows the novel to be written as such. Yet even as *Galápagos* refines the way time had been used in *Slaughterhouse-Five,* so does *Bluebeard* move to make an even greater temporal flexibility possible by even less complicated means. Although the specific number of years covered in this new novel adds up to only fifty or so, there is an immense range of development within that period: the professional lifetime of an important painter and the development of a major movement in art history, abstract expressionism. Within this range of events the narrator, Rabo Karabekian, himself displays the essentials of the style's broad range of painters: Jackson Pollock's swirls and drips, Willem de Kooning's action of paint on the canvas, Franz Kline's broad sweep of gesture, William Baziotes's eerie biomorphic figures, Hans Hofmann's push and pull of blocks of color, and above all Barnett Newman's minimal presence of a vertical line and Mark Rothko's ability to make such presences glow in a quietly but persistently spiritual way. Complementing this universe of talent and style within himself is Karabekian's command of memory, by which his narrative is able to move effortlessly from the 1930s (when he is trained as a commercial illustrator) to the present (when he is a presumably failed master on the verge of reclaiming his art with a final masterpiece), with depictions of the entire history of abstract expressionism along the way.

What Rabo Karabekian most admires in abstract expressionism is its steadfast refusal to act as an arbiter in "the Supreme Court of Good and Evil" (p. 140), sanctioning certain styles of behavior in the way that realistic fiction does (a reminder from *Breakfast of Champions*). Such a purpose had been proposed to Karabekian by his instructor and master, a famous illustrator whose own art has made a fatal error with regard to time as well. His painting is realistic:

> But he lacked the guts or the wisdom, or maybe just the talent, to indicate somehow that time was liquid, that one moment was no more important than any other, and that all moments quickly run away.
>
> Let me put it another way: Dan Gregory was a taxidermist. He stuffed and mounted and varnished and mothproofed supposedly great moments, all of which turn out to be depressing dust catchers, like a moosehead bought at a country auction or a sailfish on the wall of a dentist's waiting room.
>
> Clear?

Let me put it another way: life, by definition, is never still. Where is it going? From birth to death, with no stops on the way. Even a picture of a bowl of pears on a checkered tablecloth is liquid, if laid on canvas by the brush of a master. Yes, and by some miracle I was surely never able to achieve as a master, but was achieved by the best of the Abstract Expressionists, in the paintings which have greatness birth and death are always there. (pp. 83–84)

Bluebeard, narrated as Karabekian's autobiography, traces this idea thematically, not just through the birth and development of this style of American art but in the painter's own rediscovery of his talent and its application to the key subject of his life, the quiet aftermath of the Dresden holocaust. Like Vonnegut's own artistic rendering, *Slaughterhouse-Five*, Karabekian's masterpiece is at once figurative and abstract, timely and timeless. But also like Vonnegut's earlier novel this testament is completely fluid in its narrative use of time, the only obvious distinctions in chronology being Karabekian's awareness in such transitional comments as "Back into the past I go again, with the present nipping at my ankles like a rabid fox terrier" (p. 54). In the mind of a living human being there are really no hard and fast distinctions between past, present, and future—just a seamless awareness that both Karabekian's painting and narrative can capture.

In *Hocus Pocus* (New York: Putnam's, 1990) Vonnegut combines the style of a protagonist's narration (as in *Bluebeard*) with the framing device of an editorial introduction (as in *Mother Night*) to produce a novel that draws upon his full array of techniques to structure the void of an ungraspable yet very threatening subject matter. The most immediately political of Vonnegut's fictive works, it draws on the most emphatic topics of his essays and speeches from the late 1980s: that through personal greed and economic neglect the country is being allowed to dissipate into a nonexistence of decayed infrastructure and foreign ownership, while similar laziness and cupidity have allowed the planet itself to be ecologically abused to the point of imminent destruction.

These ideas, while not impossible to articulate, are very hard to take seriously. The hardest test for the imagination, after all, is to conceive of its own lack of being. Imagine the imagination imagining, as Samuel Beckett would say, and you have a nice Chinese box effect of continual, unending action; but trying to imagine that the imagination doesn't exist yields a dead end of conceptual blankness. This very state of events is what makes such catastrophes as cultural bankruptcy and global destruction possible, Vonnegut believes, for it is virtually impossible for a culture to imagine its dissipation and for the human race to consider the inability of the earth to support its existence. As a subject, therefore, the impending dangers of *Hocus Pocus* are an even greater challenge to the writer than the unspeakable nature of Dresden.

Vonnegut's solution for structuring this void is one an engineer might propose, and it certainly reflects his army training in that field and the styles of thought he moved in during his years working as a publicist for the General Electric Research Lab. The device is one of parallel structures, and it works to elucidate the subject of an unimaginable future by means of algebraic equation. Not just thematically, in the sense that the narrator, Eugene Debs Hartke, can make comparisons between America's involvement in Vietnam during the 1960s and Japan's foreseen economic presence in an America of the year 2001, but structurally, especially in the way *Hocus Pocus* is read: throughout the novel an almost subliminal series of correspondences are drawn so as to create a narratological universe binary in design, with every aspect of the present situation mirrored in an opposite (yet with suggestive affinities) another world away.

There is, for example, the peaceful little college on one side of Lake Mohiga and the massively foreboding state penitentiary on the other, as opposite as can be until the narrative collapses their distinctions thrice over: by moving Hartke's teaching job from one to the other, by having the prisoners invade and occupy the college, and finally by having the college reconstituted as a penitentiary itself. On a more subtle level there are linguistic devices which unite disparate sections of the narrative, such as the phrase "in the shadow of Musket Mountain when the sun goes down" (pp. 91, 101, 133, et al.) which is repeated verbatim but for radically different circumstances: as the trysting place of lovers and as the burial grounds of executed hostages. Scores of other such phrases knit the narrative together, conditioning the reader to make associations—to make connective structures— where reason would not otherwise suggest them. By this means is Vonnegut able to elucidate a subject matter that itself defies the imagination. In order to engage even the subliminally inattentive reader's participation, the story ends with the narrator proposing a mathemati-

cal formula for answering one of the tale's persistent questions; working it out prompts one more parallel between Vietnam and an economically occupied America, but more importantly forces the reader to dig back into the narrative among the more subtle parallel links in order to come up with the numbers needed.

Throughout his career Vonnegut has used the most familiar materials to construct his interpretive system of correspondences and differences, and it is this system—and not its purported subject—that remains the central feature of his work. Consider how many purported subjects either never appear at all or are deconstructed to the point of nonexistence: the revolutionary spirit in *Player Piano,* which intends to smash the machines but only conspires to rebuild them through inveterate tinkering; the determinations of the Rosewater fortune, which is dribbled away in a cruel mockery of philanthropy and then, via an acknowledgment of universal paternity, disbursed into nothingness; and of course the bombing of Dresden, which in all of *Slaughterhouse-Five* never happens.

What fills the novels, however, are structural elements of Kurt Vonnegut's autobiographical experience, from Indianapolis and the Great Depression to his current life in New York as a major author. Through it all he has spoken to his readers in that most familiar of voices, his own. It is how he advised young people to write in an advertisement prepared for the International Paper Company (a manufacturer of tools for structuring the void) and collected in *Palm Sunday* (New York: Delacorte Press/Seymour Lawrence, 1981). "I myself find that I trust my own writing most, and others seem to trust it most, too," he advises, "when I sound like a person from Indianapolis, which is what I am" (p. 79). By coming back to that essential core for his structures, Kurt Vonnegut creates a bridge over the void of existence that isn't himself. In so doing his autobiography successfully structures that void and yields readable fictive narratives.

3

Ritual:

Max Apple's

History of

Our Times

As Kurt Vonnegut takes the otherwise unknowable self and from its elements constructs a system for interpreting the world, so
does Max Apple approach the history of our
times, which would otherwise remain an ineluctable subject, and transform it into something writable and therefore understandable. In doing
so he follows Vonnegut's example in several important ways.

Americans do require richly colored symbols, three dimensional and
juicy, Vonnegut tells one of his own characters in *Breakfast of Champions*. Max Apple understands this need, and by taking advantage of
the great technical innovations forged by Vonnegut, Richard Brautigan, and the other writers who came to prominence in the 1960s, he
has made the practice of such ritualization a major concern in his
work. In the 1960s reality was attacked on two fronts: philosophically, by the Deconstructionists who forswore all attempts at identity
in favor of systems of difference (in which only the system and not the
thing itself could be known), and sociopolitically by developments in
the culture itself, which outstripped all definitions and threatened to
make no sense at all.

As proposed by Vonnegut, who saw that a functional system of
symbols could be much more satisfactory than possessing a reality no
wise person would want anyway, history itself serves best not as a
fetish of the world, which controls us, but rather as a ritualized
operation that is the creature of its practitioner. Such is the plot of
Bokononist religion in *Cat's Cradle*, and Max Apple's talent has been
to transpose that style of understanding to the component factors of
contemporary American life. Reading through his pair of novels and
two short story collections one encounters plenty of objects from our

real historical world, from Walt Disney and his plans for a magical kingdom to Howard Johnson and his chain of ice cream parlors and motels. But in the fiction writer's hands, as opposed to the historian's, they become not the determinants of our destiny but rather pliable figures in our enactment of it—and because we ourselves (through the fiction writer's agency) write the script, that enactment becomes a ritual for understanding ourselves and our roles in social life.

One challenge faced by Max Apple's predecessors in the 1960s was the way history, with all its signs and symbols, intruded upon the present and often stripped it of its sense of reality. For young people in the counterculture, life at times turned into theater, as costumed like archetypal cowboys and Indians they rehearsed American destiny in the strobe light of drugs and psychedelic music. Political leaders invoked an even larger Destiny, and novelists such as Norman Mailer and John Updike were overwhelmed by their own deep symbolism in trying to come to grips with these events. In terms of artistic reaction to our culture, such familiar forms as the conventional novel of manners and uncontested realism virtually disappeared. Whether for good or for bad, and whether lasting or temporary, the social and political changes in American culture during these years had outstripped fiction's customary ability to respond. Ken Kesey found the most apt locale to be a madhouse (*One Flew Over the Cuckoo's Nest*), while Richard Brautigan threatened to disappear into pure language (*In Watermelon Sugar*), and Kurt Vonnegut was tempted by his Tralfamadorians to fly off into outer space (*Slaughterhouse-Five*). Here were writing techniques equal to the disruptive times, but how could one structure the seemingly chaotic content left behind?

Devising such strategies has fallen to Max Apple and other writers associated with him in style and belief—among them, Tom Robbins, William Kotzwinkle, Susan Quist, Gerald Rosen, and Rob Swigart. For these writers history is not an intrusion, but is instead an example of the intertextuality that lends substance to our lives. No life is a blank tablet; from birth onward we are inscribed with the history of our times and of ages previous, and since most of this inscription is in the form of other texts, the best response is to incorporate them within our own enactments of meaning, our own lives of fiction. Consider Max Apple's young manhood: its more common aspects saw the commercialization of America through restaurant and motel chains and any number of other franchised outrages, while politically he came of age quaking at President Kennedy's missile brinksmanship and worrying that the FBI's J. Edgar Hoover himself would arrest him for his antiwar protests. But rather than flee from these intrusions into an insane asylum or outer space, Apple includes them as part of his own text, a text as author he can control: the Howard Johnson's motels of "The Oranging of America," the political cast of characters in his novel *Zip,* the Disney brothers in "Walt and Will" (collected in *Free Agents*), and eventually this whole mélange of American ritual intertexts in his novel *The Propheteers.* Once safely inside his own fiction, they are manageable and productive. As their obvious artistic manipulator, Apple can now incorporate them into the ritual of American life—a satisfying, juicy, three-dimensional ritual which Vonnegut has said we as readers need.

Virtually all of Max Apple's talents and techniques are present in the title story of his first collection, *The Oranging of America* (New York: Grossman, 1976). The formulation itself implies a sense of ritual: of something happening on a national scale, and not just to the political and social entity of "the United States" but to the symbolic concept of "America" at large. There is an intertext of historical characters and real-life incidents to Apple's story, with a man named Howard Johnson motoring across the country in the 1930s, 1940s, 1950s, and 1960s, choosing sites for his restaurants and motor lodges. Of course this fictional Howard Johnson, with his little eccentricities and visionary powers, is not *the* Howard Johnson who pioneered the idea of motel chains in America. Yet in Apple's story as in American business practice itself, the historical image is deliberately maintained as an informing presence. Consider how when a faceless corporation bought the Kentucky Fried Chicken chain of carry-out restaurants the actual founder, Colonel Harlan Sanders, was retained as an advertising symbol, with his goatee, white suit, cane, and other Southern mannerisms copyrighted as trade marks. The lesson for business practice is here much the same as for postmodern fiction: while the personality (or palpable subject matter) of a huge corporation can be neither written or known, a fictionalized projection (based on all those differences— who in normal American life walks around with a goatee, white suit, and cane?) can, all the more ironically because the real person with all these attributes who once ran the business is now a complete fiction. Yet it is by fictions rather than reality that we know Kentucky Fried Chicken, and so the world. Max Apple's Howard Johnson is just such a creature of the intertext, and the America he travels in his specially equipped limousine is an equally fabulous version of the country being transformed by franchised commercialization during these same years.

Apple's attitude toward these changes is not at all negative. Indeed, he sees Howard Johnson's innovations as helpfully transformative, as with the aid of his trusted associates he changes the concept of the motel room "from a place where you had to be to a place where you wanted to be" (p. 16). To accomplish this Mr. Johnson must make changes in the physical design of motels and in the geography of their locations, with a special style of restaurant and menu to accompany this new reality. But it is Max Apple's role as a fiction writer to case these developments in ritual form. Johnson travels less as a motorist than as an ancient deity aboard a flying chariot; he does not simply plan a route, but in Biblical language "he contemplated the map and saw that it was good" (p. 5); ice cream flavors are adopted or rejected not according to marketing surveys or scientific testing but according to the tastes of his chauffeur. As Howard Johnson and his secretary Mildred Bryce are driven across the country, their journey takes on epical proportions, especially in the way it transforms their own time and space: "the reality of her life, like his, was in the back seat of the limousine, waiting for that point at which the needs of the automobile and the human body met the undeviating purpose of the highway and momentarily conquered it" (p. 7).

Here is the key to Johnson's business method and the heart of Apple's ritualized short story. In the world of Howard Johnson, lives are measured in rest stops. So attuned have he and his colleagues become to the business of travel that their existence revolves around the locations between places where normal people live: the transitional periphery of others becomes their own center, an inversion of the country's normal text and a ritualization of travel behavior. In almost constant motion themselves, their need for occasional stops becomes significant, "sensing in themselves the hunger that would one day be upon the place" (p. 7). Here Howard Johnson will disembark from his complex limousine, leaving its shelter to face the naked landscape, waiting to feel the secret vibrations which will tell him where his fellow Americans will feel compelled to seek rest. And so up goes a Howard Johnson Motor Lodge and Restaurant, the former with its king-size beds and pulsing showers, the latter with its butterfly shrimp and many exotic flavors of ice cream. But from whence comes the idea for the distinctive bright orange roofs? For this key point Apple takes us to another intertextual figure, a poet who has contributed much to America's legend and has become a legendary figure himself: Robert Frost. Years before, he had been Mildred's college instructor, and later in his fame he welcomes his former student and her employer to his home. Following this visit, the two business visionaries spend an hour at sunset overlooking the New Hampshire hills celebrated in Frost's poetry. Recalling that experience, Mildred invokes her own moment of the holy and spectacular:

> And we stayed on that hilltop while the sun began to set in New Hampshire. I felt so full of poetry and . . . of love, Howard, only about an hour's drive from Robert Frost's farmhouse. Maybe it was just the way we felt then, but I think the sun set differently that night, filtering through the clouds like a big paint-brush making the top of the town all orange. And suddenly I thought what if all the tops of our houses were that orange, what a world it would be, Howard, and my God, that orange stayed there until the last drop of light was left in it. I didn't feel the cold up there even though it took Otis so long to get back to us. The feeling we had about that orange, Howard, that was ours and that's what I've tried to bring to every house, the way we felt that night. Oh, it makes me sick to think of Colonel Sanders, and Big Boy, and Holiday Inn, and Best Western. . . . (p. 18)

With Mildred's story of the orange roofs Apple's attitude toward his material is clear. The mixture of Robert Frost's high poetic vision with the marketing strategy of orange-roofed motels is ridiculously comic, yet in a gently teasing rather than bitterly satiric way. Apple does not judge his characters and their values. Howard Johnson and his chain of motels are not good and not bad—they simply are there, and to take them into measured consideration Apple devises a ritual. Rituals are prescribed forms which when applied to the unknown help us at least to articulate our feelings. Why Americans should patronize motel chains in such great numbers is indeed mystifying—variety is the sought-after spice of life, and the dull uniformity of one motel exactly like another, night after night and mile after mile, seems a poor lure. But succeed they do, and in "The Oranging of America" Apple makes up some reasons why. In his subplot is his clearest reason. Mildred fears the decomposition following death and so arranges to have her body frozen; there is even a chain of Cryonic Societies to do this, just as handy as the Lawrence Welk condominium she lives in and the new Walt Disney amusement park where Howard wants to locate one of his motels. "And if you did not believe in a soul, was there not every reason to preserve a body?" (p. 15). What else are these motels and restaurants except temples for the body's comfort? With the soul making no demands, attention to the material world takes on ritual proportions; and where once the ideal of a universal church provided mankind with a standard of consistency throughout the varieties of existence, now in our secular age the orange-roofed accommodations of Howard Johnson fill all needs.

The Oranging of America includes nine other stories which extend this same mode through contemporary American culture. President Gerald R. Ford is here in "Patty-Cake, Patty-Cake . . . a Memoir" as the narrator's buddy "G. R." from Grand Rapids, who even in his days as a national leader depends upon a double-batch of fried donuts from back home to achieve his perfect equanimity. For most Americans today, "Cuba" means "Fidel Castro," but for previous generations the island meant "baseball," and in "Understanding Alvarado" Apple joins the two in a story of a White Sox slugger who has retired to political and military fame in revolutionary Cuba and who now must decide whether or not to compromise his independence by seeking his baseball player's pension from the States. Characteristically, Apple turns his plot on a ritual: a former Sox teammate who has traveled out to Oriente Province to persuade Alvarado agrees to let the question be decided in a duel with Fidel Castro—not with weapons, but with bat and ball, a single hit off the Premier giving U.S. baseball the right to bring Alvarado back. Alvarado umpires, and signals Castro's victory with a called third strike. "Actually," he admits to his wife, "the pitch was a little inside. But what the hell, it's only a game" (p. 94). Both diplomatic maneuvering and baseball are indeed games, and ritualizing their common elements once more helps Max Apple articulate a problem which might otherwise go unsolved.

Odd little wrinkles of American popular culture fill entire stories. Television game shows are given the treatment in "Noon," where the narrator explains why he has committed an on-the-air murder of TV's leading host. "My beginning and my end is television" (p. 124), he explains; for although his own situation is an extreme example, with his parents having been married on a show called *Bride and Groom* and his own capital offense taking place again on live TV, the average American household with its fourteen daily hours of exposure to the medium surely risks being consumed by it. For the show's master-of-ceremonies, Larry Love, our narrator has the greatest professional respect. "I thought that it was camp that I liked *Trade or Betrayed.* I was wrong. After several years of watching, I realized that Larry is not kidding. He appears daily like the sun to remind you what the world is" (p. 130). Because of his success at "promising electric comforts if you exploit your greed," he has become the culmination of television, a virtual symbol in himself. Sending the man's statistics to an astrologer, the narrator learns that Larry Love is a perfect match for Abraham Lincoln—"How's that for irony. Honest Abe and Slippery Larry, the two faces of a coin" (p. 131). And so the impulse toward assassination is inevitable, once their roles are ritualized. "Go ahead if you must," Larry tells the narrator when he sees the gun, "in this business time is money." And as the narrator admits, "The last impulse I have toward him is one of admiration, the kind of admiration you have for something so wholly conceived that its essential nature is untouched by experience. Larry is encased like a zoological specimen" (p. 135), just as Lincoln in his marble monument has become a ritualized figure immortal in his presence yet unknowable by Americans today in any other way.

There are lighter notes among the stories in *The Oranging of America,* but even then Max Apple's practice of ritualizing events refines the world until a voice emerges which can articulate meaning. "My Real Estate" follows a fourth generation Texan whose roots reach back to the Alamo (his great-grandfather accepted General Santa Ana's invitation to leave) and whose family farm has given way to the massive structure of the Houston Astrodome. Through various accidents he is adopted by the Dome's builder and owner and is placed in line to inherit back his family's land with the Astrodome included, complicating the ambitions of the realtor who has courted him sexually with hopes of a small bungalow sale. Most of the story has been devoted to the Dome's magnificence as a sports arena and pop-cultural temple, but Apple concludes with his narrator's realtor-girlfriend bubbling over with plans for their new acquisition:

> "No," she says, "first we'll evict the baseball team and the conventions. We can make a big profit on these auditorium seats. Then

we'll put up modern bungalows, just the kind you wanted. They'll be close to downtown and have every convenience. There's room here for dozens. Even the outdoors will be air-conditioned. We'll put good private schools in the clubhouses and lease all the corridor space for shops and supermarkets. A few condominiums down the foul lines," she says, "and a hospital in center field. The scoreboard will be the world's biggest drive-in movie." (p. 119)

Extrapolating the ridiculous from a ritualized reality just a shade less absurd, Max Apple's vision in these stories supplies the themes appropriate to our age. Lest our modern fetishes become routine and therefore invisible to us, he pushes them that final extra mile into silliness, letting us see our shabbier habits for what they are.

Zip (New York: Viking Press, 1978) employs themes and techniques that have made Apple's shorter fiction successful. Like Mildred's speech to Howard Johnson and the realtor's expressed vision, this first of his novels is written in the form of second-person direct address. This makes it a self-conscious text, the message from the self-apparent writer (a junk dealer turned boxing manager named Ira Goldstein) to his intended reader, the middle-weight fighter Jesús Martinez who is ever-present as the pronoun "you." As a text, it answers another text, the book of Martinez's own memoirs which have been critical of Ira's handling of the fight game. "Let me steal nothing from you, Jesús, my middle-weight," Apple's narrator begins. "The story is all yours, conqueror of the roped-off ring, hero of the dusty Third World streets" (p. 1). The mode of address is self-consciously mythic, echoing the epic poetry of ancient Greece and Rome. But its subject is the world of faded glories in modern day Detroit—its minority ghettoes, immigrant neighborhoods with ancestral memories reaching back to Czarist Russia, and the hopes for fame in the Motor City Arena.

A ritualized reality pervades Ira Goldstein's life as an intertext: the Lithuanian folk-customs of his grandmother, who frets over his behavior and spins out superstitions galore. Hence Ira grows up trusting that the angels are selecting a future wife for him, who will in turn bear the great-grandchild his grandmother can see and thus guarantee herself a place in heaven for eternity. His mother's first love and, ten years after his father's death, still her husband's rival—Solomon the junk dealer—is caricatured in the grandmother's vision as pure evil. Hitler and Solomon, Ira grows up thinking, these are the scourges of the world. But much of contemporary reality also yields figures who become textual characters in Ira's young life: the moral fortitude and righteousness of the FBI's J. Edgar Hoover, the radical politics of Tom Hayden, and the ideological presence of Fidel Castro—all of whom make appearances in Ira's own adventures and advance the action.

Zip begins with Ira learning that one of his junkyard employees has boxing skills and undertaking his management and training for a career in the ring. But young Jesús is not your average athlete: the adopted son of a famous New York Communist organizer, he has grown up in the rarefied atmosphere of party work and doctrine, sincerely believing that one day Gus Hall will be president of the United States and that nondomestic property will be reappropriated along Marxist-Leninist lines. In Ira Goldstein's world, however, Jesús is caught between two worlds: " 'The most versatile Communist ideologue since Trotsky,' Fidel calls you, but to Grandma you remain the dangerous basement dweller, the shadow between herself and her family, the evil eye on her grandson's future" (p. 24). "Get some zip" (p. 2), Grandma urges, worried that her grandson is halfway through his twenties and still without a girlfriend. His one sexual experience has been a piece of intertextuality, as the apocalyptic mood of the Cuban missile crisis has prompted his date to experiment orally before the holocaust begins. Now, in the highly charged atmosphere of 1966 his gestures toward a romantic affair are complicated by the coed's radical beliefs and his own uncertain political and economic status.

From all of this, Jesús Martinez will be a saviour and redeemer. Yet Ira's use of him is flawed, providing the basis for subsequent political texts. Exploitation and greed, setting one man against another—these archetypes of human existence are brought to a point in the ritual of prize fight promotion, in which Ira literally "owns" Jesús Martinez. "The beginning of the alienation of labor is the management by one individual of the affairs of another individual" (p. 12), reads one of these texts, and in retrospect Fidel Castro will say of young Martinez that this was his "immersion in the cauldron of capitalism" (p. 22). Apple's literary tactic has been to take the sometimes abstract issues of competing economic systems and flesh them out within an easily understood ritual, and for this purpose boxing is the perfect vehicle. In the ring Jesús is a natural; but outside of it he can articulate its political dimensions and provide the arena for a debate between the two systems' leading figures: for American capitalism, J. Edgar Hoover, and for the socialist side, Premier Castro. *Zip*'s subtitle is "A Novel of the Left and the Right," and the political squaring off of these two larger opponents finds its more personal image in the rhythm of the fighter's left and right jabs. In the process Ira discovers just what "zip" really is: "The mind and the body together, this secret pleasure" (p. 40) which is in fact an analogy for Max Apple's writing technique.

This sense of zip creates the novel's style. Using metaphors which lend a physical sense to abstract concepts, Apple writes sentences which breathe a life of their own. His immigrant grandparents not only carry the past with them, but "Their only child, Frieda, they raised like a memorial candle to the old ways" (p. 45). When Frieda herself approaches her millionaire first lover ten long years after her husband's death, "He hugs her as if she is a cashier's check" (p. 51). In similar manner Apple allows Ira Goldstein as his narrator to invest the novel's characters with both personal presence and larger historical dimension. When the FBI's director, J. Edgar Hoover, is called in on the case of the fighter's communism, Ira is caught between the sense of Hoover's unfriendly posture toward sixties radicalism and the memory of "how right he was in all the TV dramas of my youth" (p. 86). Thus Hoover is neither fact nor fiction but rather a blend of the two, bred of Ira's fantasies as he grew up in an America recovering from the gangster years of Prohibition and the Depression and facing Cold War threats in the 1950s. Within this vision Ira can recognize the director's mythic role. "Hoover is timeless, solid," he notes. "He is not only the green of floor safes, but also of mail boxes and telephone company service vans. He exists to make sure that everything actually works" (p. 90). By hoping that Hoover recruits him as a spy, Ira is seeking to enter as a character himself the text of his imaginative life. The fact that he is a draft resister and therefore a felon in the director's eyes means little when ranked beside the power of a young boy's fantasy. In such comparisons Max Apple is telling us where he thinks the truly important things in life take place.

What transpires in *Zip* touches base at times with reality, but its essence is that of ritualized fantasy. Jesús and his party-contact kidnap J. Edgar Hoover and fly him to Cuba as hostage for a symbolic world middle-weight bout, with the young fighter turned ideologue representing communism and the U.S. champ representing the American system. Televised worldwide as a propaganda spectacle, it is in fact an invention much like Apple's baseball duel in "Understanding Alvarado" as all of the gamelike metaphors for political struggle are for a moment turned into physical reality. Howard Cosell, himself a media institution, is the ringside commentator. Hoover scores the fight from a basket suspended above the ring, himself part of the show. After many stunning rounds, Jesús is defeated, but not as a boxer and certainly not as a political adversary. Instead, Apple's language has characterized the American champ as a machine, a harvester of wheat, and Jesús Martinez as the bounty of Nature. Begun as athletics and transformed into politics, the fight of the century concludes as pure ritual, articulating the deeper motives that lie behind all these mundane concerns.

As motives, however, they are not necessarily more real, especially in the sense of a validating subject matter. Apple's talent is for showing how his world's intentions are in fact a network of arbitrary forms, the utterly conventional nature of which makes them such an artistic joy to deal with. Even as matters threaten to get out of control, Ira can tell his girlfriend that his involvement with Jesús and all his intertexts "was the first chance I ever had to really do something in the world" (p. 156), because in managing the boxer's career Ira has for the first time managed what passes for reality, that system of signs and symbols deconstructionists say constitutes the world. The greater part of Apple's work is given to this manipulation of popular forms, but within their ritualization is a more specific understanding of how it all comes down to language. There is always room for a Grace Paley-like simile ("the Communists who popped up like flares in Grandma's long and lonely life," p. 170) and a Richard Brautigan-style metaphor ("Jesús has trained outside of his body. He is standing now in the realms of pure spirit. He is a block of marble and Tiger Williams some petty Michelangelo chipping away at him," p. 181), which extend the gap between tenor and vehicle in a way that enhances the individuality of each while creating a third entity, the startling nature of the comparison itself. Life may be a text written by others, but Apple's narrator has learned how to impress himself upon it, becoming part of this quarter century's encyclopedia of popular forms by learning how to manipulate them himself. From the junkyard he has ascended the whole world's stage. His grandmother should be happy, since he now has "zip."

Apple's second collection, *Free Agents* (New York: Harper & Row, 1984), exploits this larger ritualization and the closer textualization which accomplishes it. As befits a maturing author, this collection is at once more self-confident and more daring than much of his previous material, beginning with the volume's dedication and disclaimer which reveal the starkly autobiographical nature of the stories which follow. But for Apple autobiography is not a straight path to narrative. Instead, action must take its form in ritual, and for this to happen the self must find a textual form. Apple's children, more prominent than ever since he has been widowed, aid this process, for they are indeed the "issue" of Apple's own fatherhood who now enjoy their own status in the world. These children, Jessica and Sam, populate many of the stories, as does the lost image of his wife, Vicki.

The volume opens with "Walt and Will," a story in which the Disney brothers are paralleled to Howard Johnson and his associates in "The Oranging of America"; its epical nature is revealed in the story's original title, "Disneyad," as it appeared in the *American Review #26.* Here Walt's genius as a cartoon animator is complemented by his brother Will's talents as a businessman. From studying anthills Walt knows that cartoons draw their life from the simplest fact of small-creature life: there is no stillness, all is motion. A mouse is always a mouse, he insists; the ploy is not to picture a human imitating a mouse, but to show a mouse trying to be a man. Will, however, insists that all this action must be leading somewhere: to the principle of pure motion he adds the direction of plot, of *story,* and thereby completes the dimensions of textual narrative. Will's ambition is to make feature cartoons of Bible stories, but the development of an epical amusement park (with such realms as Fantasy Land, Tomorrow Land, and Main Street U.S.A.) yields an even better effect. "Man is only dust and time and spirit," he boasts, "but Disneyland can make him strong as an angel" (p. 14). America has never had a national monument, an attraction equivalent to Notre Dame or the Taj Mahal. "We'll build a center for America. A place where you can stand and move the world from" (p. 15), he exclaims, and in the ritual nature of his plans Max Apple finds a structure for fiction.

The stories which follow in *Free Agents* implement Apple's own plans for creating narrative from his biography and textualizing himself. In "Bridging" he uses a Girl Scout term (for a girl's progress from Brownies to the Scouts) to dramatize his own relationship to his suddenly motherless daughter. His own religious practice of maintaining a kosher diet is explained in "Stranger at the Table," which is again a matter of ritual, here made concrete in his own life-habits: "Kosher, you see, is not a style. It is an ancient, powerful, unyielding code. It is a way of ordering the world, an unconscious systematic recognition of the price we pay to eat flesh. It begins in the biblical prohibition against seething a kid in its mother's milk and is reinforced by the taboo against eating the living being or drinking blood" (p. 74). Within this ancient structure the narrator struggles against the contemporary world, whose dining habits make it just short of impossible for him to practice his religion. "I do it in spite of all the difficulties, simply because it seems right," he confesses. "One of the sublime biblical lines is God's definition of himself: 'I am what I am.' So are we all" (p. 75). Other stories ("Business Talk," "Help") find him adopting a wife's narrative voice in order to show the world from her perspective, fighting out of domestic life to forge an identity in business and learning that even threats to her remaining home life can be resolved through strictly professional forms. In "Eskimo Love" he as storyteller confronts the loss of his wife directly. Here it is significant that it is *his* sense of loss which dominates the story, as he becomes an alienated being who must be chided, "why don't you stop pretending you're an Eskimo or a hermit; why not rejoin mankind" (p. 149). When he's out ice-fishing, his wife makes an unexpected appearance, which Apple keeps deliberately peripheral: "When the line tightens I tilt on the ice; even a gentle tug can pull you in when there's no good place to stand. I reach for the slippery fish but it's only Vicki. She was in the area, she got entangled in the line. Not a bite, an accident. I see her frozen lips, her fish eyes. I cut her loose. We have already had our last words. Some deaths are final" (p. 144). As with his kosher habits in the earlier story, Apple's strategy here is to provide a form by which his wife's absence can be textualized, made into an object of narrative rather than remaining as a loose cannon cast about on the decks of his emotional life. As such, the story becomes a success as his narrator's life is put in order.

Complementing the biographical stories are fictions in which Apple makes a text of himself: his internal organs striking for autonomy, demanding the right to choose their transplant hosts ("Free Agents"), mixing an old recording of his bar mitzvah and a school recitation with his Uncle's Yiddish tunes, all being played in the radically different context of a party for urban Blacks ("Blood Relatives"); and most obviously in "An Offering," in which a prospectus is drawn up for the sale of common shares in Max Apple, Inc., "a reliable supplier of stories, novels, and essays fit for mass consumption" (p. 179). Throughout *Free Agents* runs the sense that words are his only tools. And what complicated tools they are, for unlike notes of music or daubs of paint, they carry a world of reference with them. "He can't help it if the language is a kind of garbage collector of meanings" (p. 137), he complains. Yet there is a voice that comes from the silence, from the "otherness" beyond the everyday use of words, for which he can strive—the otherness of ritual meaning. And this becomes Max Apple's style of fiction. "Take comfort in sentences," he advises his readers. "To you they're entertainment; to me, breath" (p. 91).

Such breath is the medium by which the author confronts and interprets the strange new world around him. In Kurt Vonnegut's case the measure of that breath has been the elements of his autobiography. Max Apple turns not to his own life but to the ritualized experience of his country—the autobiography of America itself, as the country forms images and proposes narratives in order to make sense of how its fortunes have developed. His short stories choose a single element—Fidel Castro, Howard Johnson, Walt Disney, or some other figure that the culture has blown up larger than life as a way of reckoning with existence—and then run that image through a ritualized narrative, testing it for meaning as it is recovered for "normal" experience (such as seeing Howard Johnson not as a motel-chain name but as a singular human being scouting locations for his stores). Apple's first novel, *Zip,* is similarly short and focused on the cultural and especially political themes of the 1960s. *The Propheteers* (New York: Harper & Row, 1987), however, expands Apple's approach to much larger proportions, its longer length and wider breadth of action encompassing greater areas of geography and spans of history. In *Zip* J. Edgar Hoover had met Fidel Castro, but in this later work Apple's entire panoply of ritualistic personages interact for an epic of popular culture.

Each specific action in *The Propheteers* draws on ritual to achieve this epic proportion. A piece of Florida real estate, for example, encompasses three interests of especially grand dimension: Ponce de Leon's fountain of youth, a base for launching astronauts to the moon, and finally as Walt Disney's second great (and perhaps greatest) amusement park, itself encompassing America's mythic past and future ideals. Howard Johnson and Mildred Bryce make a special guest appearance from their own story, replete with the master's ability to know the land "the way the Indians must have known it" (p. 5). Walt Disney shows up with his own key ingredient, the theory of animated motion, but this larger narrative also reaches out to include C. W. Post and his mystic devotion to the good of cereal and Clarence Birdseye at work in the Soviet Union searching for a way of fresh-freezing produce and encountering a Marxist view his industry hopes to answer ("Fruit," a Russian official complains, "by its nature, is against the interests of the working class. It is expensive to transport and has a high spoilage rate. The only workers truly able to enjoy it are the growers or those close to the market. Yet they rarely taste this fruit of their labor because the market value makes it necessary to ship fruit immediately to the tables of the rich. . . . The people need bread, not frozen berries" [p. 101]).

Max Apple's language elevates these subjects. As in "The Oranging of America," Howard Johnson "contemplated the map and saw that it was good" (p. 3); two hundred pages later another character behaves in similarly Biblical fashion, as "C. W. Post had seen the world and pronounced it fit for Grape-Nuts" (p. 201). In each case the author mixes levels—the loftiness of religious expression, the lowliness of maps and brand names—yet evokes a common purpose in the ritualistic function of these acts, from Howard Johnson decreeing where Americans will find rest in their travels to C. W. Post determining the food with which they begin their day. Howard Johnson behaves like an Indian scout, chewing the grass and marking a spot with his urine; at one point his actions coincide with the end point of the Lewis and Clark trail. Other locations call to mind Jericho, Mecca, and other holy places; in his actions he evokes the identity of Abraham Lincoln and adopts his functional importance for those with whom he's involved. He is seen choosing the same spot, for the same reason, as Ponce de Leon: "Any place this comfortable," the explorer contemplates, "has got to be close to paradise" (p. 121). C. W. Post is anointed by his father Abraham with the oil from a Winchester rifle; Walt Disney builds on the scale of the Incas and the Mayas and is fueled for this purpose with the ritual beliefs of millions: "More kids know the Mouse than Jesus Christ. We could build a religion, a college, an atom-powered village—anything we want" (p. 156). Coming upon Orlando, Will Disney (the developer) feels how Columbus must have felt on discovering the New World, while his brother's genius for animation has made him the equal in art history to Michelangelo and

Leonardo. The fact that the Disneys' interests are running counter to those of C. W. Post's daughter only make the struggle more epic, for which their culture provides another handy form: "Was she the kind woodsman and Walt Disney the cursed prince, and was there some secret thing they had to do before he could emerge to his full strength and energy?" (p. 251). Meanwhile, C. W. Post has hired Salvador Dalí to steal and replace with cereal-enhancing replacements the world's great masterpieces of art. Hardly anyone in this novel's action is anything less than a personage of worldwide notoriety, but even more instrumental to Apple's narrative is that they rarely interact with anyone other than at their own exalted level.

How the mythic worlds of Howard Johnson and of Walt Disney intersect accounts for half the novel's action. Although each is famous for his own reasons—Johnson for understanding the country's needs when it travels, Disney for not only animating Mickey Mouse but for realizing that Americans need a national shrine—Apple's narrative perceives a more fundamental relationship between their activities: "Howard Johnson is the means, Walt Disney is the end" (p. 35). Here is the binary opposition between transiency and stable location, between travel and vacation. Especially for the latter two terms, people make major distinctions, but it is Max Apple's genius to figure this contrast by means of the two symbolic personages and their ritualistic activity. And so when Howard Johnson is tempted to emulate Disney's method, his assistant strongly objects. Sociologically Disneyland shares functional characteristics with the nightmare—and nightmares are just what their restful accommodations have been dedicated to avoiding. Moreover, "When you can't see your car from your bedroom something strange happens. . . . You lose some faith in a building that takes you away from your vehicle" (p. 110). A Howard Johnson's Motor Lodge and Walt Disney World are therefore quite different parts of the American ritual and it is dangerous to combine them. As the former comprises stillness, the latter embodies motion, even though there is motion involved in the larger context of travel and a certain amount of stillness in staying at Disneyland for a week or two (Howard Johnson himself notes with envy how his rival has transformed the unit of one night's stay into seven or fourteen). However, each practice is a ritualized form, and therefore there is great narrative resistance against mixing them.

When Margery Post finds herself involved with Howard Johnson in resisting Walt Disney's plans for a new Disney World in Florida, she is able to articulate the importance of these names and the meaning behind them:

> It was an odd coincidence, she realized, that she and Walt Disney and Howard Johnson were human beings, that big business had taken their names without wholly taking them over. Even Walt Disney was just a man.
>
> Maybe it lasts exactly one generation, she thought—actually in her own lifetime, Margery had watched the Post name disappear into generality. The company was no longer Post Cereals; that had become General Foods, and she certainly was not General Foods. When Howard and Milly were dead they would become General Motels, and after the Disneys, there would be General Amusement Parks. All the big industries eventually became general. Howard Johnson and Walt Disney, by their very success, were insuring that they too would become anonymous. Nobody thought of C. W. Post anymore when they ate Grape-Nuts, and her father's hot drink, Postum, had become a general name, like coffee or tea. (pp. 264–65)

What Margery describes is the transparency of language itself, by which the materiality of signifiers disappears into the easy referentiality of what they signify. Here the real, historical, and personally present C. W. Post becomes a sign for his cereal and drink, but within a generation yields his full identity to a signifier; a name becomes a word.

Max Apple understands this effacement and regrets the immediacy and physicality, not to mention the human dimension, that is lost in the process. His ritualization of popular history, however, restores all of those senses. When he writes about himself, he expresses this same belief in ritual existence and the benefits it offers. Introducing his anthology *Southwest Fiction* (New York: Bantam, 1981), he explains why he has left his native Michigan to live and work in the radically different and distant environment of Houston, Texas, where "The reality of the plains and the desert reminds us that the central episode in American history, the settling of the frontier, is still happening in the Southwest of the 1980s" (p. ix). Here is the natural world for Apple's style of fiction:

Fiction, by its very nature, is universal. Neither culture nor language is an ultimate barrier, and time, which mocks so much human effort, barely scars the story. The imagination is securely settled in the timeless, but the body lives in times and places. When those times and places are fictionally created, they are never obscure; they are rooted in truths beyond history, yet they occasionally illuminate the historical. . . . The whole is always too much to see. (p. xix)

And so in Max Apple's fiction the uncomprehendible whole is broken down into constituent elements and recast as ritual. As ritual, it is under control by the writer and is given in articulated fashion to the reader, who can experience the waking dream of America made real.

4

Comedy:

Gerald Rosen

and Rob Swigart's

California

In Kurt Vonnegut's autobiographical structurings and Max Apple's ritualizations of history, one element remains constant: that of comedy. And not just comedy as laughter, although both can be screamingly funny. In each language follows the pattern of comic form, depending on distance rather than tragic identification. Although Walt Disney and Howard Johnson are brought together, the humor of this situation is that distance remains a key factor—not just distance from each other, in that the two figures were unlikely to have ever met, but in the distance between their businesses and their persons. Was any lodger ever checked in by Howard Johnson or welcomed through the gates of Disneyland by Walt himself? About as likely as meeting Mr. IBM or Mrs. AT&T. And as for the specific materials of literary art, the startling effectiveness of simile and metaphor—most obvious in Richard Brautigan's work but a hallmark of virtually all innovative fiction rooted in the American 1960s and 1970s—it is the distance between tenor and vehicle that becomes the key factor, with the resultant identity serving only as a reminder of how far the reader has been brought along.

As structurings of the void progress into the 1980s, comedy becomes only more important, beginning with a rhythmic joy of inflected language and triumphing with pure comedic effect, unsupported by autobiography, ritual, or other fabrications bridging the void of subject matter. In the novels of Gerald Rosen and Rob Swigart, humor itself becomes a structure—Rosen's *The Carmen Miranda Memorial Flagpole,* for example, is generated and then held together by the device of classic one-liner jokes, while Swigart's plots deconstruct the more serious businesses of biology and physics by using the properties of DNA and quantum mathematics as cues for detective and science fiction strategies. But in all cases the basic impulse can be found within the use of language itself, with theme reserved as something the problematic nature of subject matter makes secondary.

As far back as the 1950s this need for language to resolve the messiness of thematic concerns was evident in the work of a writer no less serious than Saul Bellow. Fully half of his books qualify as comic masterpieces, but chief among even these would be *Henderson the Rain King* (New York: Viking Press, 1959), a work whose delight in the physical joy of language influences Swigart and especially Rosen a third of a century later. Audiences who have seen Bellow in less than even temper can appreciate how the language of his fiction provides such service even in his moments of professional dismay, as happened on the occasion of his reading at Northern Illinois University in 1970 with a scene that could easily appear in one of Gerald Rosen's novels a decade or two later. The two English department professors scheduled to meet him for dinner hadn't shown up, and so Bellow stood by himself in the student union, watching a rerun of "Lost in Space" while hundreds milled around, wolfing popcorn and wondering who he was. Two hours later, across town, a couple of graduate students thought they saw him at the Shamrock, finishing a beer and a radar-range sandwich and asking the bartender where University Hall might be.

They knew it was Bellow for sure when he stormed past the flustered professors, marched out on stage, and without a word of introduction opened a paperback of *Henderson the Rain King* and started reading.

"What made me take this trip to Africa?" he began, beet-red with anger but also weary with resignation. The combination made for a perfect voice, a voice that would skim over countless catastrophes of theme to find solace in the palliative language of comedy. Yet the underlying tone of exasperation with events made it a perfect combination. "There is no quick explanation," he answered his own question, setting up the hilarious paragraph to follow. "Things got worse and worse and pretty soon they were too complicated."

Too complicated for treatment as a subject, but an apt provocation for structuring the void with comic language. Within a few pages Bellow had the audience in stitches and began laughing himself, although the story wasn't what you'd call *funny*. "When I came back from the war," he read, "it was with the thought of becoming a pig farmer, which maybe illustrates what I thought of life in general."

Henderson, the character who fears death will "annihilate" him, that "nothing will remain, and there will be nothing left but junk," plots a comic revenge on his family, on his Hudson River Valley estate, and on the world, all of which lose their staying power as vexing subjects in the flow of comic language that wondrously washes them away, just as it was cleansing and removing Bellow's anger at having been stood up before his speech:

> I took all the handsome old farm buildings, the carriage house with the paneled stalls—in the old days a rich man's horses were handled like opera singers—and the fine old barn with the belvedere above the hayloft, a beautiful piece of architecture, and I filled them up with pigs, a pig kingdom with pig houses on the lawn and in the flower garden. The greenhouse, too—I let them root out the old bulbs. Statues from Florence and Salzburg were turned over. The place stank of swill and pigs and the mashes cooking, and dung. Furious, my neighbors got the health officer after me. I dared him to take me to law. "Hendersons have been on this property over two hundred years," I said to this man, a certain Dr. Bullock.
>
> By my then wife, Frances, no word was said except, "Please keep them off the driveway."
>
> "You'd better not hurt any of them," I said to her. "Those animals have become a part of me." (pp. 20–21)

As with the generations of comic writers following him, Bellow's technique is rooted in difference: the startling contrast between the lovely estate and the pigs (the word itself being repeated thrice in less than half a sentence), between the delicate objects of culture and the animals' crude behavior, and most of all between the narrator's manner of level description and the chaos his acts are unleashing. In the process the threatening enormity of theme—the meaningless void into which Henderson has seen the postatomic world thrown—becomes less of a problem. Though never solved in itself, it provides the narrator with an occasion to talk, and as in most Bellow novels he manages to talk his way out.

Though Henderson is distinguished as being Bellow's sole WASP protagonist, his reliance upon voice to palliate the world's woes fits in with an important strain of comic narrative: the rhythmic inflections of Jewish-American speech, which from Philip Roth's and Bernard

Malamud's earliest novels of the 1950s to Gerald Rosen's work of nearly half a century later proves useful for structuring the void of unacceptable subject matter. Consider Roth's Neil Klugman fretting over his relatives in *Goodbye, Columbus* (Boston: Houghton Mifflin, 1959). "Life was a throwing off for poor Aunt Gladys, her greatest joys were taking out the garbage, emptying her pantry, and making threadbare bundles for what she still referred to as the Poor Jews in Palestine," he admits early on. "I only hope she dies with an empty refrigerator, otherwise she'll ruin eternity for everyone else, what with her Velveeta turning green, and her navel oranges growing fuzzy jackets down below" (p. 7). Or the resignation Malamud projects into the character of Morris Bober in *The Assistant* (New York: Farrar, Straus & Giroux, 1957), who, brought down by a robber's blow, thinks only of its appropriateness: "He fell without a cry. The end fitted the day. It was his luck, others had better" (p. 25). Subject matter here is transposed into song; the music is either hilariously funny or comically bitter, but the instrument in each is the human voice, moving fiction closer to its basic component, words—words which in these two examples have outstripped any referentiality to subject by colliding in radical difference, whether of a life on earth motivated toward consigning things to their deaths or a luck which could be better.

Like Max Apple in the 1970s, Gerald Rosen and Rob Swigart inherit the world of 1950s anxiety and 1960s disruption as already made, a text already written, a verbal presence in their own lives which must be read and articulated in the process of stating their own fictive vision. But once a mode for working with such intertextuality is found, as with Apple's ritualization of history, the field is open for gamesmanship with language and carnivalized play with previously authoritarian texts, with Bellow, Roth, and Malamud's comic language as a useful voice whenever needed.

Rosen and Swigart are linked in geography and emigration as well as in style, for each was born in the East and moved West to find successful careers while living in the San Francisco Bay area and locating much of their fiction in California. Their early novels show the same revolt against the confines of tradition and employ many of the literary devices pioneered by Vonnegut and Brautigan as a way of liberating form from restrictive content. Subsequent works find them discovering the California landscape and transformed social and cultural reality and are followed in turn by still newer novels that develop a formally stylistic approach from this new attitude toward content. By the end of the 1980s the void that had been such a threatening force in their first novels is no longer a factor—not because it has been replaced with an alternative content, but because in structuring that void each writer has found a truer subject for his work.

In these terms Gerald Rosen's transformation has been particularly dramatic. Born in the Bronx, son of the owner of a liquor store located in the troubled neighborhood of West Harlem, he pursued an education in the sciences and business—a bachelor's degree in electrical engineering followed by an M.B.A. from the Wharton School of Business—while taking time to manage the family business. A stint as an officer in the army followed, then more studies (beginning the transition in his career) leading to a Ph.D. in American Studies from the University of Pennsylvania.

His first novel, *Blues for a Dying Nation* (New York: Dial Press, 1972), follows a young protagonist named Jake, whose induction into the army is almost literally a drowning, as his basic course in swimming expands as a metaphor for the submergence of basic freedoms by an increasingly militarized nation. The America Jake narrates is an extrapolation of various political and social tendencies of the Vietnamized U.S. of the 1960s, and his actions—both as a character and as a storyteller—are an attempt to come to terms with what he perceives as that void, characterized in the novel as a virtual erasure of the American ideals Rosen would have studied in his doctoral courses at Pennsylvania. As a narrator, Jake struggles to fill the void, inserting actual newspaper clippings on the country's mayhem into the book's pages and interspersing "commercials" and "bulletins" as a television broadcast might in order to give a greater sense of impending doom. As the novel's title suggests, the story is essentially apocalyptic but for reasons of form as well as content: the country may indeed be out of control, but Rosen's narrator cannot find a way to express his own comments. Like Kurt Vonnegut in *Slaughterhouse-Five,* both Rosen the author and Jake the narrator must not only struggle with their materials but eventually learn that the art of that struggle constitutes their true subject.

The subject of military America actually effaces itself throughout the book. Like "the Combine" in Ken Kesey's *One Flew Over the Cuckoo's Nest,* its actions are elusive and sinister, yet never liable to be pinned down and called to account. And like the military itself in

Joseph Heller's *Catch-22*, the rhetoric it does employ is absurdly contradictory yet internally faithful to its own fractured logic. Together with his narrator's emulation of the method of *Slaughterhouse-Five*, Rosen's debt to the innovations of sixties fiction is obvious. Yet as much as the military-industrial complex haunts the mood of Kesey's novel, and as much as an awareness of Vietnam pervades the World War II described by Heller and Vonnegut, none of those works addresses itself to this problem of the 1960s directly. That becomes Gerald Rosen's task in *Blues for a Dying Nation* and signifies his rank in the progression of contemporary American fiction.

The novel itself works a double transformation: of domestic America into a Vietnamized landscape and of fiction itself into an equally reflexive act. The army in this case acts at home as it does abroad, shelling villages at random as a way of establishing its presence and authority. Meanwhile Jake, who has given up plans for jail or Canada by submitting to the draft—in the hopes that his promised assignment to hospital work will allow him time and scope for writing a novel— takes a self-conscious approach to his work, as in this exchange of dialogue:

> It's Edith in the doorway.
>
> "Jake . . . I know you won't believe this, but there's a phone call for you. . . . It's your mother, Becky."
>
> "I don't believe it."
>
> I turn back to the car and Edith shouts, "Jake! I'm not kidding. It's your mother. There's a telephone on the kitchen wall and your mother's waiting to speak to you. It's long distance, Jacob."
>
> "But. . . . But how did she get the number?"
>
> "That's what *I* asked. All she would say was, 'Don't think it was easy, young lady. Don't think it was easy.' She's kind of excited, Jacob. You'd better speak to her."
>
> "I won't."
>
> "But Jacob . . ."
>
> "I won't speak to her. She can't follow me around like this."
>
> "But . . ."
>
> "Edith, I *won't* speak to her! There'll be no Jewish mothers in this novel!"
>
> "Jake, be serious."

"I *am* serious. I will *not* answer that phone. The Jewish novel is dead. She was born too late."

"Jake . . . she's waiting."

"I'm not kidding."

"But I have to tell her *something*."

"Tell her to call Philip Roth. Tell her this is *my* novel and she can call all day, she's not getting into it." (pp. 42–43)

As the army blasts apart his life, Jake tries to restore its order with art, based on J. S. Bach's method of composing music as an attempt at replacing his progeny lost to childhood illnesses. Such an attempt is indeed a structuring of the void, as Jake explains to a friend: "Each grave must have seemed like a hole in the universe that Bach felt he had to fill with the substance—with the structured solidity—of his music. And he *would* fill it. Only to have another kid die" (p. 67). Yet his enemy has structures too, making him feel like he's trapped in a horror movie "Or a painting. . . . A Guernica" (p. 90).

The narrative action of *Blues for a Dying Nation*, then, becomes a contest between competing systems, Jake's and the army's. This action wends its way through a landscape of semiotic forms—of Abe Lincoln's cabin or Tom Sawyer fishing from a bridge and other signs commonly used for the American experience. Jake's most personal confrontation is with his swimming instructor, Cal (or Cali, nicknamed for California, itself a sign of America's manifest destiny), who is a direct descendant of General (later President) Zachary Taylor, archetypal representative of the military's role in directing domestic American life. Here the contention is enhanced by their sexual roles; significantly, it is Cal who exploits hers as a weapon in their contest. Jake travels to Concord, invoking Thoreau's transcendentalism as an antidote (fearing that Cal's ability to keep him in a perpetual state of excitement will wear him down to death much sooner), but this journey provides the chance to expound a larger, more systematic understanding of how the American ethos developed from Puritan New England:

The presence of evil was real to their poor fathers, but they were the first generation of Americans to come into contact with the Asian teachings of being and nonbeing. Evil became lack of being, and this made sense to a nation of progress worshippers who could almost see the evil disappear as the nation brought its wilderness under control. And this was the beginning of America's denial of the existence of evil altogether—until recently that is. (p. 220)

Now, because evil is presumed to have infiltrated the country by means of the counterculture's civil disobedience and contrary life-style, the army seeks to obliterate it just as the colonists obliterated the forest, the presumed heart of darkness and evil. The army's transformation seems ahead of Jake's, particularly when he finds himself turning a stripper he meets into "a kind-hearted whore from a nineteenth-century novel" and reflects that "maybe I can't make it in this world because I'm lost in the wrong century and maybe that's where I belong, in a nineteenth-century novel, and maybe I'm a fictional character myself, the product of the fevered imagination of some frustrated author who can't fit into the modern world and who belongs in a nineteenth-century novel himself" (p. 308).

Jake's momentary doubt in himself is eventually overcome by realizing that everything is not, as he fears, imagined; there is a reality beyond his fantasies—a reality that fantasizes *him* as an enemy. And so he assumes the mythic role of an American Indian pursued by the army. Yet this very mythos insures his defeat; the only room for triumph is in the realm of art, for it has been an artistic role that he plays.

With its heavy burden of history, politics, and myth, *Blues for a Dying Nation* shows Gerald Rosen poised at the threshold of California comic: sensing the need for a transformation, but unable to accomplish it in terms other than surrender to historical inevitability, a transformation in which the rival system's structuring has prevailed. In his next work, however, Rosen incorporates that structuring not as a theme but as a formal device in itself, thereby allowing himself to set the novel's terms rather than simply reacting to them. The structure of *The Carmen Miranda Memorial Flagpole* (San Rafael, California: Presidio Press, 1977) employs a geographical transposition to serve this larger structure: an automobile journey from the closed, inhibiting confines of the East (here New York City, but recalling the history-laden Massachusetts of *Blues for a Dying Nation*) to the more open, creative possibilities of northern California. As a thematic device, the novel's approach is hardly original; indeed, it draws on Jack Kerouac's *On the Road,* just as its structural format recalls the East-to-West, closed-to-open, confined-to-creative movement of Ronald Sukenick's *Out.* What qualifies Rosen's novel as a genuine innovation are the specific techniques used to move the narrative between these two points. As the character Jerry tells the story of a cross-country trip with his older brother, Jack, that telling is structured by a seemingly unending series of jokes. Not deftly intellectual humor or sophisticated comedy, but self-apparently embarrassing one-liners with pratfalls worthy of the corniest baggy-pants comedian. The jokes themselves are justified as Jerry tells them: "Anyway, my parents were in the iron and steel business. My mother ironed and my father stole. (Ratatatat—Bong!) No, seriously, I apologize. I'll try to stop. I can't help it. I love old jokes. Jokes were the only art form we had in the Bronx" (p. 2). What is taken from their New York City childhood, then, is not a content but a form, and exercising this form allows them to structure the void not just of their urban childhood but of the immense distance they must travel across the middle of America (a region bi-coastal citizens characterize as a vast desert or as "fly-over country") and of the blank page awaiting them in Sonoma County, California.

The novel itself begins as a joke, ostensibly a "Psychiatric Introduction" drafted by Gerald Rosen's analyst as a warning to readers. The interpretation advanced here is that Rosen, although a fiction writer, considers his characters to be real, either as autobiographical projections of his own life or as a figuration of the older brother he wishes he really had. "He's lonely," we're told. "He wants a brother. He fantasizes that a brother exists. And then he attributes his crazy pranks to his imaginary brother as a way of not facing up to what he himself has been doing" (p. iii). What characterizes the preface as a joke itself is that it is signed by "Dr. S. Freudenberg, M.D.," who proves his own existence by drawing on the proofs of Shakespeare's Shylock and Descartes's reasoning ego, expressed as "I am, dear reader; I swear to you, I am. Pinch me, do I not hurt? Cut me, do I not bleed? Don't pay your bill to me, do I not sue?" (p. v). What functions as seriousness, however, is the fact that the narrator's brother, whether projected or not, is a novelist, much like Jake Klinger in *Blues for a Dying Nation.* In Rosen's new work, however, his narrator can stand both inside and outside of this process, writing his own book (*The Carmen Miranda Memorial Flag-*

pole, which by the doctor's transposition becomes Rosen's novel) yet also able to comment on his brother's fiction, thus doubling the dimensionality of Rosen's first novel.

It is how Jerry regards the world, however, that shows the emergence of Rosen's California comic reorientation. As he and his brother pick up a car to transport to the West Coast, Jerry notes a behavioral detail about a woman in the agency's Times Square offices: her "very perfume exudes *Daily News*" (p. 7). As the tackier of New York's dailies, this newspaper can be said to characterize its readers—lower education, lower economic status, a lesser sense of taste and image, and so forth. But here the comparison makes a much larger leap: not to her general personality but to her perfume. In Rosen's device metaphor and synecdoche are conflated into a single act, inviting the reader's own sense of play with the figures of rhetoric. Together with Jerry's jokes, the narrative is spiced with such comparisons throughout its journey. Even the destination is characterized in especially vibrant terms, asking the reader to combine metaphors from such distinct fields as sociology and mathematics. "California is America squared," Jack explains to his brother. "One last 3000-mile chance for people who couldn't make it on their first trip to the new world" (p. 14). Crossing this America, Jerry and Jack vitalize its local mythos, drinking regional beers in order to support the local breweries, recalling the "Gothic cathedrals" (p. 16) of their youth which took form as the old ballparks in Philadelphia, Pittsburgh, Cincinnati, and St. Louis. These early examples, however, imply a certain doom to at least part of their project, for the little breweries disappear one by one, while Shibe Park, Forbes Field, Crosley Field, and Sportsmans Park are only faded memories, their Gothic intricacies replaced by anonymous, virtually uniform concrete donuts, just as the individual charms of local beers have been washed away in the mass markets for Budweiser and Miller Lite. The impetus for their discovery of a "new" New World, then, is given added lift by seeing how the failed nature of the first great discovery has crept across the land in a parody of their own journey.

A dauntless optimism characterizes the brothers' trek. They're anxious to embrace each region of America in the best aspects of its mythical form, to the point of rolling into Chicago exclaiming, "HOG BUTCHER TO A NATION! LOOK OUT GENE AMMONS! LOOK OUT NELSON ALGREN! LOOK OUT LOUIS SULLIVAN! LOOK OUT ANDY PAFKO! HERE WE COME!" (p. 16). From Carl Sand-

burg's poetry, Gene Ammons's jazz, and Nelson Algren's fiction to the
skyscrapers of Frank Lloyd Wright's teacher and the popularity of the
Cubs' right fielder, Jack is eager to embrace the city's best, just as his
own intent is to find a new land, Opteema, to replace the confines
of New York, the ultimate twentieth-century city whose restrictions
cause him to call it "Pesseema." California, with its beaches populated
by a new, free generation of surfers, is his new ideal.

More bright language sparkles along the way. A disapproving wait-
ress looks "as moral and legal as a Lincoln Continental" (p. 19); when
some boring tourists spoil his view of the Grand Canyon, Jack does his
impersonation of Martha and the Vandellas doing "Heat Wave," scar-
ing them off; and when California itself turns out to be as clogged with
capitalistic and middle-class paraphernalia as New York, Jack transposes a standard Buddhist prayer to his new surroundings:

> I take refuge in the Buddha.
> I take refuge in the Dharma. [The law; the Way.]
> I take refuge in the Sangha. [The Buddhist Monastic Order.]
> (p. 101)

Each time he enters the local supermarket, Jack kneels down in front
of the plate glass windows facing the checkout aisles and intones:

> I take refuge in the Buddha.
> I take refuge in the Dharma.
> I take refuge in the Safeway.
> (p. 102)

The play on "refuge" and "safeway," enhanced by the alliteration of
"Sangha" with the grocery chain's name, is linguistically effective. But
behind it all is Jack's belief that it is only by its systems of signs,
linguistic and other, that a society marks reality—creating, in other
words, what passes as *its* version of reality. As the postmodern semi-
ologists have pointed out, each society classifies objects in its own way,
and this way constitutes the very intelligibility it grants itself. The
Safeway routine, by interfacing two differing systems, is an attempt to
point out the workings of that practice and lobby for an alternative
view.

Jack's extended practice of this belief has yielded a novel—*The
Majority Hallucination,* the elements of which seem much like Rosen's
own *Blues for a Dying Nation.* His theory is that readers must be

shown "that reality is only a shared hallucination of the majority of people at a particular time and place—a kind of 'novel' in which they've come to live—and that they've gotten themselves into a bad novel that doesn't make them happy." The practicing novelist's job is "To give people a better hallucination in which to live" (p. 23). His strategy is in accord with semiology, realizing that "the way to change the world is to change the way we imagine it" (p. 24). Jack is disappointed, of course, that his first novel hasn't changed the world—just as Rosen's *Blues for a Dying Nation* didn't. But some novels do—consider how Joseph Heller's first book gave the world a new phrase, "catch-22," operable for describing a new view of warfare. And so *The Carmen Miranda Memorial Flagpole* continues tracking Jack's efforts, which have now graduated from the archetypes of American Studies to the signs of poststructural semiotics.

When Jack's attempt to write a new work fail, Jerry is bidden to take over. The former will simply live, while the latter will write about his efforts: "Call it, 'The Carmen Miranda Memorial Flagpole,' and write about what we're doing here, and see what happens" (p. 205). Gerald Rosen's actual novel of that title, a title that comments on the group's ritual of stringing up an enormous sombrero decorated with fruits and vegetables, succeeds to the extent that it fulfills Jack's own abilities as a writer of texts and an actor in life: "Change the space we were in by using only words" (p. 147). He knows that the Yiddish speakers of the old Eastern European urban ghettoes had only two names for flowers, and none for wild birds, so little a part did flowers and birds play in their lives. Within the subject matter that Rosen's novel describes, Jack never succeeds in transforming the world. His pranks and pratfalls, intended to be instructional, backfire into destructive nonsense. But what of his brother Jerry's role? Like the allusion to the Abstract Expressionist painters, who threw away the canvas and framed their palettes (p. 115), Jerry learns that his own act of writing is, as an act of structuring, more important than the void over which it is spread. Although Jack fails, Jerry succeeds in writing, to the point that it is now what he does most of the time. For the moment he has lost his brother, but he shouldn't be hard to find. As Jerry advises his readers, "You won't have any trouble recognizing him. He looks a lot like me" (p. 176).

Significantly, once Rosen is himself established within the California comic style of the creative play of language and the generative force of

social signs, he can turn back to elements of his East Coast heritage
and revitalize them not as subjects but as factors in structural play. A
transposed version of his family's business is combined with Rosen's
new vocation and relocated in San Francisco's Mission district in *Dr.
Ebenezer's Book and Liquor Store* (New York: St. Martin's Press,
1980), while the author's childhood is addressed through the device of
memory in *Growing Up Bronx* (Berkeley: North Atlantic Books,
1984). The former is a testament to San Francisco's sensuosity, as the
book's initial chapters are awash in the sights, sounds, and smells of
lush sexuality and exotic cooking. The liquor store itself distills these
elements into vehicles of primary communication: books to stimulate
the mind, booze to stimulate the body. There's room for sly jokes, as
when a well-heeled woman comes to the checkout with a copy of John
Kenneth Galbraith's *The Affluent Society* and a bottle of Chivas Regal,
but behind the operation is "Dr. Ebenezer" (real name, Ben Gross), a
former physicist who is ministering to society's mental and physical
needs in atonement for his work on the atomic bomb. The store itself
serves a focus for three additional characters: Dr. Harry Lutz, a drop-
out professor from Columbia University who now clerks in the store;
Wendy, a Japanese-American who lives with the tragedy her people
suffered as internal exiles in World War II; and Treena, a former Las
Vegas showgirl whose poetry and intellect are located deep within an
abundant sexuality, a figurement of the book and liquor store itself.
The novel itself is essentially plotless, a refinement of California comic
in which the characters are able to respond to the texture of life itself
without the need for an artificially construed action. Their responses
are, in turn, a natural justification for Rosen's language, the richness of
which is displayed in such casual encounters as remarking how his
characters experience a jazz recording: "They sit, quietly, listening to
John Coltrane explore the architectonics of velvet" (p. 154). Their
awareness, suffused by good literature, music, and wine, transforms
reality; the commonness of a Taco Bell fast-food outlet becomes something quite different when Treena calls it "Pachelbell," after her favorite early baroque composer. She plays with language itself, considering
crossing a peach and a zucchini to get a "peachy-keeny" (p. 171). What
action there is traces Dr. Ebenezer's movement from Treena to Wendy,
from a frustrated and disappointing love to one that is returned and
fulfilled. But none of it is accomplished with hollow moralizing of the
type found in Thomas Pynchon or William Gaddis, whose spokes-

men advise readers to keep cool but care or to love and do what you will—both of which statements have led critics to advocate a shallow humanism in their works. No such imposed meanings clutter the California comic approach of Gerald Rosen, which lets the texture of experience speak for itself.

That *Growing Up Bronx* turns back to Rosen's adolescence in New York is not surprising, for it reflects the refinement apparent in most innovative fiction within the 1980s. In fact, it anticipates by three years a move such hardcore innovators as Clarence Major, Steve Katz, and Ronald Sukenick would make in 1987 as each published works drawing on his youth: *Such Was the Season* (Major's novel set in Atlanta, where he was born and spent the first part of his childhood), *Florry of Washington Heights* (Katz's memoir-styled fiction about his teens in upper Manhattan), and *Down and In* (Sukenick's account of the attraction of the underground scene in Greenwich Village during his late teens and early twenties). On the surface it would seem that just as Rosen returns to the East, these writers refocus on an object for their writing; can this be construed as an attempt not to structure the void but to fill it with a previously inaccessible subject matter? The answer is both yes and no, for while a certain style of object now exists in their work, it is not apprehended or employed in the traditional sense of objectivity. Postmodern semiotics defines the object as *what is thought* in relation to *one who thinks*; here the unitalicized words are as crucial as the two factors between them, for subject matter is now being understood not as an entity in itself but as a relational system, perhaps even the system of differences the deconstructionists insist is the only workable definition of what exists. Rosen's transposition of the California comic style to such inherently Bronx material is the best example of how this relational approach to subject matter works, because the author's technique is now seen as less a matter of region than a state of mind.

The achievement of *Growing Up Bronx* is its discovery that any subject matter, any object in the world, is not so much a thing in itself as it is a factor which generates a relationship—and that while the object itself may not be seized, the relationship can. This discovery takes place for the writer and the reader alike, for in Rosen's novel the subject matter proves not to be his narrator's adolescence per se, but rather the narrator's relationship to one of his aunts—Aunt Rose, originally a teenage bobby-soxer still sporting her baby fat (and skipping high school in favor of the movie houses at her bus transfer), but all too soon a ruined and disappointed woman, whose body and mind have been ravaged by the sense of time into which the young narrator must grow. The pattern is repeated in Clarence Major's *Such Was the Season,* to the point that the aunt in his story takes the role of narrator herself, reflecting on the young man's return to his scenes of childhood; for Steve Katz the ostensible object, Florry O'Neill, dies before his narrator can complete his story, which turns out to be an attempt to locate his present-day adult self in relation to this year in his adolescence forty years before; Ronald Sukenick, writing about an East Village he never had the courage to embrace until well into his manhood, sees the underground life as avuncular, something half a generation beyond him yet influencing his life nevertheless. The life of Rosen's narrator, Danny Schwartz, has abundant action of its own, from observing his parents to interacting with his neighborhood, from watching the conduct of World War II abroad to shagging batting practice for the New York Giants and being batboy for a day. But these narrative particulars only make sense in relation to the innocence-to-experience action followed by Aunt Rose, whose presence not only puts these smaller acts into perspective but allows the narrator a basis for his viewpoint. Structurally, it is similar to Jake's view of the army and its Vietnamized America in *Blues for a Dying Nation,* to Jerry's reaction to his brother's fantasies, and to the omniscient narrator's appreciation of Dr. Ebenezer and his cohorts in a sensuously supercharged San Francisco. But more than these first three novels *Growing Up Bronx* applies the technique to what in conventionally realistic fiction would be called a stable and coherent object. Here, however, that object becomes not a thing in itself but a differential construct of what is thought in relation to one who thinks, focusing the text on the author (and hence on the reader) more than on the ostensible subject—which is, after all, ultimately ungraspable.

Complementing Gerald Rosen's refinement of the California comic approach to structuring relations with his subject matter is Rob Swigart's extension of the same technique to the expansive possibilities of mind. Like Rosen, he is a transplanted academic from points East (Cincinnati and Buffalo). His fiction, however, begins squarely within the style of California comic; instead of moving from East to West in terms of technique and then reembracing a certain eastern topicality as has Rosen's, Swigart's work begins with life out west and then moves off the continental limits Rosen's characters had presumed to be the last resort of possibilities. Where *Carmen Miranda*'s Jerry and Jack see the terminus in Sonoma, and while the characters in *Dr. Ebenezer* tend to see each topographic feature of San Francisco as "America's last hill" or "the country's last stretch of flat land," Swigart's people follow the action all the way to Hawaii, delve into the ocean itself to talk with dolphins, travel through outer space and into the afterlife, and eventually devise a narrative structure within the artificial intelligence of computers.

Rob Swigart's doctorate is in comparative literature (SUNY-Buffalo), and much of his research has been with computer technology and innovation, but his novelist's career begins with *Little America* (Boston: Houghton Mifflin, 1977), the story of how young Orville Hollinday is swept up by the concept of America as a nation of wheels, a country a significant portion of whose life is spent "inside capsules that rolled on wheels over endless interconnected ribbons of asphalt, concrete, Tarmac, from here to there and back again, in a universe that rolled on and on, though it knew in the tiny decaying orbit of every improbable electron and meson and quark that somewhere the wheel would slow to a stop, but that when it did the universe would collapse and explode and start rolling again, because it is in the nature of wheels to roll" (p. 1). Orville embraces this action by rejecting the stabilizing imperatives of his father (whom he spends the novel trying, in comic fashion, to blow up) and yearning instead for a position of stasis within motion, ideally as the proprietor of a gas pump at the world's largest truck stop out West. As the novel proceeds, a broad range of aspects of late twentieth-century American life are encountered; the father's response is always contrasted to the son's in terms of an east versus west, modern versus postmodern orientation. Where Orville Sr. seeks hierarchy, Orville Jr. embraces anarchy; purpose yields to play and design to chance; totalization, the father's image of control, becomes in the son's hands an act of deconstruction; centering becomes dispersal, selection turns into combination, depth yields to surface. What was determinate becomes indeterminate.

Little America and *A.K.A.: A Cosmic Fable* (Boston: Houghton Mifflin, 1978) are strongly complementary works, each relying on a California comic sense of vibrant language and creative metaphor in order to sustain actions that traverse, in turn, the coastal limits of America and the outer reaches of galactic space. In this second work

the protagonist is a millionaire Chicagoan named Avery K. Augenblaue who has developed an orgone-powered spaceship that shoots
him out toward the Magellanic Clouds, returning after ten years with a
message of hope for the polluted and self-destructive planet Earth. But
as Avery has learned, the message is not the medium, and so the
essential business takes place within the medium itself, which for
fiction is its component words. For example, when two characters are
overwhelmed by the Arizona heat, we're told "It seemed to fall on their
heads like a couch-sized bronze anvil, like a downpour of sticky hot
fudge, like a collapsing water tower full of boiling sorghum molasses"
(p. 62). As for more local conditions, "The Chicago air was gradually
shellacking the city with layer after layer of dirty brown, and through
the bottom layer the large and white Augenblaue Rolls Royce Silver
Cloud flowed like a leucocyte on its way to an infection" (p. 146).

The plot of Swigart's novel runs through a mad mélange of space
technology, desert-spa health clubs, underground filmmaking, and
government intrigue, all of which is smothered by a thick layer of
good-time sex. The plot weaves its way through the workings of
energy cells, adrenal glands, and termites—all linked together in an
answer to the world's problems. Tracing one's way through to that
answer is the fun of reading this fiction, and even though the thematics
can be considered lightweight, the structuring technique is anything
but insubstantial. Here Swigart shows well. The big advance of innovative fiction in the sixties was learning how to shape stories so they
would fit our expanded consciousness—before Vonnegut no writer
could compete with a child flipping channels on TV. Swigart has this
technique down cold, running six or seven stories simultaneously, so
there is no chance readers will get bored. And when these strands all
come together, the effect is overwhelming. If fiction wants to be fun, it
had better keep up with the competition of movies and television. In
this league, *A.K.A.* does nicely.

Avery's solution for the world is rather simple—just add more
love—but his techniques for doing just that make the novel quite
readable. Through it all runs the hint that the whole mad routine is
ordered by the Reichean "deeply stirring secrets of our nature," some
hidden plan which our limited vision won't let us fully perceive. If
searching for this plan doesn't get you everything, at least it gets you
something: a feeling of having walked in a style and left a track that fits
present-day experience. Conveying a sense of that experience is what

California comic hopes to accomplish: that and a sense of humor. When we laugh at something not ordinarily funny, we are certainly responding to something beyond our usual perception. Writers like Swigart say it works the other way around, too. If there is wisdom to be found, it's bound to be funny as well.

An overserious sense of heroism is just what this style of writing hopes to avoid, as an outdated Promethean vision of dominance yields to a more Protean sense of adaptability and change. Rather than rail against the banality of contemporary life, Swigart accepts it as an occasion for light humor, and his novel *The Time Trip* (Boston: Houghton Mifflin, 1979) deflates any idealistic pretensions by showing that the eternal principles of afterlife are formed in earth's own insipid image. His protagonist, a bored-to-tears housewife, finds banality even in death. Her suicide which begins this novel is as easy and efficient as sticking her head in a microwave oven. And her heaven, formed by the image of daily experience, takes place in a Holiday Inn—bland lobby, Muzak, tasteless food and all. "Cripes," complains the victim, "do they have one of these things everywhere?" (p. 3).

Her husband wants her back and uses the magic of computer programming to channel himself back through history. But in the 4,000 years of human effort from Gilgamesh to the present he finds the same clichés which haunt his own empty existence. As he searches for his lost wife in the great beyond, he has in his mind nothing but a petulant cry: "Why did you ruin the microwave oven?" (p. 4). How does a writer make fiction of all this, especially fiction which will do any good? Rob Swigart has learned the master lesson from the innovative writers of the sixties: that the real focus of a novel is the writing itself, making subject matter alone irrelevant. Swigart's advance is that his writing actually rescues his subject. As their star pupil, he shows that the literary 1960s were not in vain.

When Swigart is at his best, nearly every line he writes is charged with magic. Little matter that some of his characters are unattractive. The worse they are, as Gilbert Sorrentino has shown in his own fiction, the more fun the author can have skewering them on nicely turned conceits. Take Prudence Nisenvy, the lizardly attorney who is a party to most of the low dealings in *The Time Trip*: when she speaks, her voice is like "nerve gas percolating through stale beer" (p. 300). A cheap hotel room is furnished with neon glare, "a green ghost quoting an old detective movie" (p. 232). Language defines character and sets mood, but it is most of all interesting and entertaining for itself, and even the most naive reader will stick with Swigart's story just to see the new and funny way he describes things. A slick California suburb is named Los Cojones de Santa Teresa; the hero lives on Puerco de Esmeralda Lane. In Swigart's work nothing is wasted as a chance for inventive writing. Whether in English or Spanish, the jokes are quite literally in the words.

Swigart's novels do have plots, but they are as wackily associative as his language—indeed, the plots reinforce the language, serving as the basis for his linguistic grandstanding rather than for their own story value. In all of his novels these plots are self-reflective. The need for connections is talked about as the plots themselves connect and reconnect in all bizarre ways. But the foundation is serious, as Swigart tells us in his epigraphs. For *Little America* it is Heisenberg's Uncertainty Principle, which reminds readers that physical study yields not a picture of nature but rather a survey of "our relationship with nature." Aha, we say, the plot is in the making of the plot. The front matter of *A.K.A.* invokes Wilhelm Reich, as a reminder that our deepest thinkers still quest after "the deeply stirring secrets of our nature" even though these secrets are best found within. Barney Gamesh's own time trip in the third novel teaches him the lesson that we are all connected, beyond even time and space—a healthy corrective to the seventies solipsism which brought him his first misfortune.

But the real joy of connections is for the reader. Like Robert Altman's *Nashville,* or any other intelligent film which capitalizes on the cinematic aesthetic of our times, Swigart exploits the joy of putting things together. In all his novels six or seven things happen at once and keep happening at once until the reader exhausts his or her imagination keeping them connected. At this point the novel ends because the reader's activity has ceased. To prove that readers read for words rather than for story (they can watch the TV news for stories), Swigart makes his plot lines cohere on levels other than simple narrative. His first two novels are written in the very short chapter form developed by Vonnegut, Barthelme, and Brautigan in the sixties. In *Little America,* for example, a cake collapses at the end of chapter 57, and chapter 58 begins with a character dazed by a run-in with his boss; the reader's intelligence supplies the energy which jumps from chapter to chapter (just as in the wildly stretched metaphors) and so adds a picture to the book's ultimate collage.

The action of *The Time Trip* happens inside a computer, as apt an image for the electronic decade we've barely survived. But here is Swigart's hope, based on indigenous materials: true to his self-reflective nature, *The Time Trip* shows how computer programming itself is nothing but fiction writing and that life—as the ultimate fiction—can be what we make it. Swigart uses shady practices from our business culture to make his point. His characters finance their computer corporation by self-evident fiction, bouncing bogus checks between phony code numbers; "meantime," they say, "we get to use the money" (p. 239). Their corporation is staffed by ready-made fictional figures created as the false policyholders of a fraudulent life insurance company. Even beyond their bogus reality, fictions have their own life, as the sixties taught us: one computer biographee reclaims his life and moves in to steal the business, and even the programmers (who made him up) can't trap him.

The reality of Swigart's world, then, is completely invented. In narrowly ethical terms that is our culture's downfall, but by shifting it to the aesthetic (and hence controlling it) Swigart shows how we can find creative genius—once we realize what we have made is a fiction best governed by rules of artistic order. His fiction is more than creative; it is procreative, life-giving in the sense that our otherwise dull existence is put back under control. Run as a creative game rather than as 9-to-5 servitude, it becomes something fun to live. Rob Swigart's fiction makes us connect. His novels are two way propositions, since the reader must participate in their words and plots to get a finished product. With those connections all existence is magically alive. Without them, he shows, our daily lives are death.

In *The Book of Revelations* (New York: Dutton, 1981) Swigart completes his tetralogy, which has ranged from American popular culture through science fiction speculations and time travel to the afterlife and the past, with an extended look at alternative reality phrased within the terminology of current technique. Aesthetically, Swigart again introduces so much absurdity from the real world that his novel is forced to question itself, and the pattern of this interrogation structures his resulting fiction more ably than any simple imitation of an action might do. In the 1980s, Swigart knows, reality induces more questions than it resolves, and in terms of belief there is often doubt as to whether even fantasy can keep up with the present world. The news from California makes one wonder. Item: Dr. John Lilly, the famous and controversial neurophysician, has been talking with sea creatures. He and some friends—whom the newspapers describe as a movie star, "a famous surfer," and "a San Francisco entrepreneur"—have set up shop on the beaches north of Los Angeles. With the help of video display terminals, sonic synthesizers, and a translating computer, Lilly and his crowd will soon be chattering away with dolphins, whales, and other mammals from the deep.

If this sounds like a goofy remake of *Dr. Doolittle* with Cheech & Chong in porpoise suits and Dudley Moore standing in for Rex Harrison, don't be surprised. The saving virtue of West Coast life is that it's usually ready to make fun of itself. As soon as reality gets a little too bent, a native satirist is there to twist it more. Rob Swigart has made a career of pushing the little stupidities of life over the edge into lunacy. Junk food got you down? In *Little America* he explains why a good taco sauce is more sensual than sex. All fouled up in computer technology? Try *The Time Trip*—your bank-machine card will never feel the same. Wonder what the sea beasts are saying? *The Book of Revelations* makes the killer whale tell all.

Swigart at his best courts a challenge to the imagination. If a whale or dolphin were to speak, what would it tell us—secrets of the deep? Or a condemnation of the human behavior that has raped the land and saved the sea only as a dumping ground for garbage and nuclear waste? "Feed Jane Fonda to the Whales" read the placards at the airport; just what do the cetaceans themselves think? *The Book of Revelations* uses all the traditions of fiction to answer these questions. It takes a California think tank called Investigate the Future, a group of researchers variously psychic and managerial, and an ocean full of intelligent mammals and treats them like the characters and forces in a Henry James novel.

For a heroine Swigart chooses Cassie St. Clair, a prophetess whose inability to sort out the real from the suppositional has cost her a happy childhood, healthy adolescence, and comfortable marriage. For a plot he puts Cassie to work in future studies, where her strange ability to sense the insensible might help folks figure out what, in this crazy world of ours, is really going on. Complications? Make this all happen in a time very much like the 1980s, when "millennial expectations," triggered by an overload of cultural change, make people yearn for signs from heaven, outer space, or beneath the seas. Getting down to the nuts and bolts of such work creates a new perspective, an oddly ironic one. Do we ever really know what's going on? "There is, perhaps, and I wouldn't bet on it," one of Cassie's coresearchers admits, "some kind of external environmental reality that we cannot perceive except in fragmentary, distorted ways." So much for the world around us, which the dolphins might help us figure out. "Then there is a consensus reality, the one we all agree upon, and act as if it were all of reality," he continues. "Then there is reality as seen through the senses," and after that "mediated reality, seen on television, over the computer networks, the Dow Jones averages, statistics, and so on" (p. 85). And that's not all: there are those artificial constructs we pretend are real, which we call "models." There's psychic energy to contend with. And finally that catch-22 of the uncertainty principle, which says that our very act of looking at something changes it from what it really is.

What on earth is happening? You might as well walk out on the shoreline and ask the waves. By definition we can never know. But still we try. *The Book of Revelations* challenges all sick jokes about its subject matter to ask these supposedly unanswerable questions. In doing so Rob Swigart creates a sense of how we live in the 1980s—hurtling ourselves about in jetliners, changing planes amid reminders that what happens undersea is pertinent to the lives we live topside, and hoping that anybody new—be it killer whale, dolphin, or California novelist—might talk to us in a revealing, intelligent way.

Swigart's subsequent work of the later 1980s and early 1990s embraces structuring itself as both technique and theme. *Vector: A Thriller in Paradise* (New York: Bluejay Books, 1986) uses one of the most familiar forms for doing so: the detective novel. Only here the detection involves the basic structure of human life, DNA. Potentially criminal elements are at work tampering with it, and the book's protagonist is involved in sorting out both the suspects' actions and the DNA structure itself. The novel is a self-apparent text, a scientist's report to his editor in the form of a detective narrative—"I felt it would be more accessible this way than as a dry summary of the events; after all, this seems like fiction anyway" (p. 1). The format is recombinant DNA research, in which the researcher partially digests an organism's total DNA and then recombines the pieces with DNA obtained from a vector randomly reinserted into host cells to see what turns up—a crude way of cloning. The narrative, already enfolded by this preface (actually a text in itself, a cover letter to the editor receiving it), replicates its structure in further divisions: between the scientist/writer Charles Koenig and the detective Cobb Takamura and then between Takamura and the fictional detective he is fond of quoting as a gloss on all unfolding events, Charlie Chan. With its story action acting like recombinant DNA, *Vector* thus serves as an ideal vehicle for carrying on a narrative about some criminal skulduggery with the same process.

Part of this process involves a debate on whether limits, in the service of ethics, should be placed on genetic research. Significantly, this debate takes place in what the characters call paradise, one of the yet unspoiled Hawaiian islands, Kauai. An act of murder triggers the investigations—Takamura's, of the crime itself, and Koenig's, of the scientific process by which it has been achieved: a virus with a new kind of vector, constituting genetic homicide. Both investigations rely on structural patterns to understand the crime, which is itself an utter vacancy. Everywhere, both men encounter texts, from laboratory slides to the island's layered rock walls that "seemed to write in an unknown language the story of millions of years" (p. 115); hardly a page can pass without at least one such reference, and from them all the researchers must decode a solution. Computer technology comes on-line to help:

> "I have this hunch," Chazz [Koenig] said. "The computer will look for homologous sequences in all the DNA. If the agent is something that affects the genetic code and is found in all the victims, the computer will find and display all the matches. We can eliminate known sequences. If there is a sufficiently long stretch common to all the victims, we might have something." (p. 141)

Within such doings the elements behave according to the semiology of crime and detection. "For a secret agent—a virus, say, to survive," Koenig explains, "it must be disguised as a native, have the proper chemical marker. He must wear the right clothes, speak the right language, know the right cues, gestures, responses and so forth" (p. 201)—be able to employ all the signs, in other words, just as in a semiotic novel of manners. This violator of the DNA code must be pursued and purged, but its track is only one of many narrative paths the investigators must follow; others include an equally adept understanding of the region's anthropological codes and topographical details. But foremost is the search through DNA, for it is closest to the language structure of the novel itself: "The genetic code is made up of words. The words have three 'letters,' codons. Three bases to a codon. A series of exchanges go on; the message is read, translated, sent; proteins are made" (p. 247).

The final culprit turns out to be some illicit government research into the genetic structure of Slavic peoples so that Russians as a mass could be exterminated, better than by any atomic weapons. The prospect is horrible, but not more so than atomic warfare itself. The difference here is that the investigators cannot only uncover the crime but prevent its further use. This they do, by contriving a fiction that explains the renegade laboratory's destruction. The day is saved, and life goes on.

Rob Swigart's achievement in his next novel, *Portal* (New York: St. Martin's Press, 1988), is to assign this act of salvation to the processes of narrative itself. To make this process pure, it is cleared of all human operators and entrusted to a narrative-generating form of artificial intelligence, the computer HOMER (Heuristic Overview of Matrix Expansion and Reconstruction). The occasion is the year 2106, when a sole astronaut who had left on a distant starship probe in 2004 returns to find the Earth totally deserted. To learn what has happened he turns to the deserted civilization's computer network; within that network its storytelling machine gathers the elements of narrative and spins them until a structure emerges to explain what has happened.

Portal itself is framed as the astronaut's experience within this system, called "Worldnet" (p. 11). The adventure is self-apparently textual, thanks to the various information sources within this network whose identity is distinguished by different typefaces: local node reports, central processing commands, messages logged in by various individuals before humanity disappeared, data from the historical, medical, and other data bases (including general science and technology information), "psilink" (the proscribed area into which one character has ventured), and HOMER's own commentaries, all of which are put into order by the astronaut. He interacts with the text as he reads it, but HOMER interacts as well as "he" tells it, learning and growing in the process. To borrow a term from computer technology, the narrative is "interactive." *Portal* was first published on computer discs as just such an interactive work, and even in its hard copy form retains the subtitle of "A Dataspace Retrieval." As the astronaut explains early on, "a database is the place itself, like Homer or Central Processing. And the dataspace is what you enter once inside" (p. 28).

By means of this device the reader is put within the narrative, his or her recognitions of the differing typefaces and information sources becoming part of the act of assembling the story.

The actual plot of *Portal* is extremely simple; as a subject matter or content, it can hardly be said to exist at all, since its presence is in fact a vacancy, a void formed by the disappearance of all human life. The astronaut and HOMER are simply functions of structuring that void, fashioning a narrative explanation of how it happened and what is to be their reaction (each has to question his own sense of being—the astronaut as the last person on Earth, HOMER as an artificial intelligence whose only purpose is to serve a civilization which no longer exists). Even as a subject matter, this vanished world is described not as a solid object but as a system of relations, a supposedly utopian state in which all mankind has been organized into a "world information economy" (p. 63) in which every centimeter of the Earth's surface is constantly surveyed, every human act is measured and evaluated, and therefore every need fulfilled. But some people find this utopian perfection suffocating. The more violent among them engage in a form of combat known as "Mind Wars" (based, as in *Vector,* on genetic assault); the artists disappear into a New Age style of art known as "mozarting"; deep thinkers, however, pick up and extend the tradition of Lovecraft and Heinlein by exploring and exploiting the powers of psychic research, and it is by this last means that one of them has made the essential linkup with powers of the mind sufficient to escape the physical bounds of Earth.

HOMER's narrative is a reconstruction of this researcher's eventually successful efforts to remake humanity on the psychic level left unsatisfied by the material culture controlling life on Earth. As a narrative, it completes a full circle: brought back to life by its human inquisitor (the astronaut), it first expresses ignorance, then begins assembling individually meaningless bits of data from various disparate sources, until a narrative pattern emerges—which is first a pattern suggesting that Earth (with the computer and the astronaut) has been abandoned, but which eventually invests the two with meaning, since they are to serve as a link by which this transformed intelligence can return to Earth and reestablish corporeal form, only now fully developed as nothing less than "the consciousness of the universe, seeking to know itself" (p. 332). It is a quest, perhaps the grandest and greatest of all. But not a quest as subject matter or content, for the real action has been the interactive role of HOMER's artificial (and the reader's real) intelligence in constructing the story, which is one of the most sophisticated intellectual acts possible.

Yet the very sophistication of narrative depends upon its reader's facility with play. Like DNA itself, one of Swigart's favorite topical interests and technical devices, it is infinitely recombinant—to the point of generating the endless diversity of individuals in the human race. With the scientific aspects of such combinations established in *Vector,* and with the constituent elements of narrative sorted out (and recombined) in *Portal,* Rob Swigart is able to take his California comic technique and generate a thoroughly unintimidating story in another detective novel, *Toxin* (New York: St. Martin's Press, 1989). Like *Vector,* it is "a thriller in paradise," paradise being once more the somewhat out of the way, relatively unspoiled island of Kauai. Its function is as a blank table for the narrative, an Edenic realm innocent of the knowledge of good and evil, boasting a sometimes chartless primeval landscape open to the unfettered and unlimited structuring of those who would act upon it (and those who would decode those structurings).

The structurings themselves are an amalgamation of several distinct threads which in the narrative of *Toxin* come together to create a web of mystery and suspense. Most simply, there are business dealings, particularly those of the man whose murder begins the novel. Then there is the business of military research, involving the crash of a satellite carrying an experiment on toxins. Both businesses—land development and dangerous research—threaten the environment of Kauai, and to enhance the structure of that environment Swigart details not just its current sociology but its anthropological roots within cultural forces still operative today (inviting references to mythology and various ritualistic systems). The main characters' interests and functions within science, criminology, and the oriental martial arts provide other systems, and once more police Lt. Cobb Takamura textualizes the whole affair by quoting cinema detective Charlie Chan. In one way or another all of these systems are patterns of detection. For Swigart as author and for his audience as readers the task is to sort them out and reintegrate the pertinent features: just where do land development, military research, sociology, anthropology, biology, and criminology intersect in a meaningful way? The semantic result, of course, is held in suspense until the novel's end, according to the genre's dictates. But all along the reader is invited to play with the factors of detection, which are in *Toxin* self-apparent artifacts understandable in terms of their systematics. That the crashed satellite is itself a chimera, part of an elaborate war-games exercise contrived by the Department of Defense, only finalizes the narrative's sense of play.

A third Chazz Koenig-Cobb Takamura thriller, *Venom* (New York: St. Martin's Press, 1991), continues this play with codes and moves the action closer to that of language itself. The narrative is thick with imagery that, detached from its rationalizing system, refers less to an identifiable subject than to its own complex being, as in the paragraphs that begin Chapter Two, "Fire in the Sea," itself a title that structures a seeming impossibility:

> The sea was fearfully alive, frenzied. What looked like some mythical animal made of whorls and loops, of mounds and rolling pseudopodia, of tentacles that groped bluntly along the tortured bottom, seemed to boil with an awful, demented, impossible growth. As it rolled, it twisted inside out, heaving, groaning, subsiding, and rising again.
>
> From time to time, sheets of blue fire crackled over its surface, as if discharging electrical power over the writhing skin of the beast, as if it were dying, over and over again beneath the pressure of the water. Rings of the blue light boiled across the surface, fluttered away as the skin rolled under and turned dark, only to flash again, in jagged ripples that flashed like lightning. (p. 11)

Coming as it does after the first chapter's empirically precise (while causally undetermined) description of a murder scene aboard a derelict ship, this passage is not only unexplanatory but seems rife with contradiction. From the seven bodies discovered in the previous pages it would appear the sea is dead, not alive. And what is the nature of this life: animal, mineral, or elemental? Even the elements themselves are multiform, encompassing fire, water, earth, and air. As an underlife it is the void human actions seek to structure, and it turns out that is what's underway here as biologist Chazz Koenig dives beneath the sea to study the lava flow being sent under water by a volcano in eruption. As an action, it parallels what he himself (as a decoder of poisonous mixtures), his wife Patria (as an anthropologist unravelling the ritual practice of voudun), and Lt. Takamura (as a detective of criminal activity) will have to do in the succeeding chapters in figuring out the murders. Both areas are "a primeval environment," one as the source of life, the other as the underside of life's battle with evil.

Such researches into the depths can yield things helpful and harmful, substances medicinal or toxic, depending on the codes used to systematize them for human use. Because of this contrariness there is no real subject at hand, just a set of differences in the activity that goes on around such void. In similar manner *Venom* examines other topics, first identifying them not so much as things in themselves as relationships between others, such as the mother-son relationship that extends all the way from a group of environmentalists' view of the nurturing but threatened earth to an actual filial-maternal structure that winds up destroying itself. Such structuring of the void motivates life, Swigart knows, and also prompts the incessant popularity of detective thrillers—which are, after all, written "about" nothing but their own structuring activity.

The range of such writing is at once impressive and reassuring. From its genesis within the linguistic play of Richard Brautigan it has developed in the hands of younger writers to include a self-apparency not just of metaphor (including tenor and vehicle and the temptingly daredevil gap between the two) but of social observation, nostalgic memory, and the detective exploits of both science and crime. Its contemplation of the void within ostensible subject matters is anything but nihilistic: instead, its warmly human response is to be sympathetic to the idiosyncratic acts of human beings as they form their structures around and across that void. In Rosen's and Swigart's cases it is helpful to see how close their novels remain to the structuring substance of common American lives. From the popular culture's discovery of the San Francisco Bay area in the 1960s to the country's love of detective novels and the gadgetry of science and technology, these two writers' "subject-voids" remain at the heart of typical American fascinations. Their special achievement has been to perform an aesthetic rescue of these possibilities. A nihilistic reading of the subject's deconstruction implies that such works as *The Carmen Miranda Memorial Flagpole* and *Toxin* are no longer feasible; by allying the structuring impulse with the most natural forms of human behavior, Gerald Rosen and Rob Swigart prove that such works can serve as an accurate reading within our structuring of the void.

5

Constraint:

Gender

And what of those matters that are neither funny in themselves nor amenable to structuring by humor? Comedy is indeed the strain that runs through and unites the efforts of writers from Vonnegut to Swigart, but the unspeakable subjects— true voids—that they structure are as distant as the posturing of comedy itself. True, *Slaughterhouse-Five* involves itself with World War II, just as does Joseph Heller's *Catch-22*. But each novel is written and becomes immensely popular not in the 1940s but well over a generation later, in a decade when attitudes are so transformed that the Second World War might seem distantly remote. In a similar way Swigart's topics, ranging from DNA to astrophysics, are not immediate constraints within readers' lives.

But two political issues of more recent times are indeed constraints: the struggle for women's rights waged by feminism, and the war in Vietnam—not just the war itself, and not just the protest against it, but, as with the cause of feminism, the whole nature of how to understand it, eclipsing as it did all previous definitions of military conduct and social response. That contemporary writers have responded to these concerns with fictive devices as unique as those within the comic tradition shows how fundamental the transformation in literature has been. In each case the solution has been to take the problematics of a supposedly incomprehensible subject and use it not as an articulation of content but as a principle of structural approach. In the process voids are once again structured, and in the end there is even room for comedy where none may have been imagined before.

Yet comedy itself cannot be the immediate answer. Early failures in the literature of sexual politics and the Vietnam War attest to this, and in view of what has followed it can be embarrassing to reread novels that at publication were regarded as breakthroughs. For Vietnam the example to recall is Robin Moore's transgeneric work, *The Green Berets*; by even midwar it had become a humiliating statement, and today it reads like utter fantasy, its fully outrageous attitudes rooted in the conventionality of approach to an unconventional war. For women's issues the parallel is Erica Jong's *Fear of Flying* (New York: Holt, Rinehart and Winston, 1973), originally hailed as a breakthrough work of candor and frankness but today reading as an ill-motivated series of borrowings and posings. Like much black humor fiction of the late 1950s, its quest for pertinence is almost entirely on the level of theme, with technique lagging ten years behind (and therefore gaining its shock value by speaking so brashly about matters never before admitted to such polite dialogue). "Alas! the love of women!" exclaims its opening epigraph, from Byron, which has been used as a topic so many times that it excludes other concerns and in this case almost annihilates structure—for love, especially with its sexual equipage, is one of the few subjects that rivets attention without further work.

To the extent that rhetoric determines form, such novels end up as social realism, supposedly excusable for a work that undertakes a cause. But when cultural and political commentary surpass structure, it is the commentary that gets the front page news and textbook assignments. *Fear of Flying* is not exactly sociology, but it has accompanied *Sexual Politics* and *The Female Eunuch* into sociology courses by sticking to the situation some think sums up the American woman: "The fact was that we'd reached that crucial time in a marriage (five years and the sheets you got as wedding presents have just about worn thin) when it's time to decide whether to buy new sheets, have a baby perhaps, and live with each other's lunacy ever after—or else give up the ghost of the marriage (throw out all the sheets) and start playing musical beds all over again" (p. 3). What would for John Updike be deft comedy is here, by the need to clue the reader parenthetically, reduced to a style of social lecturing. Could that parenthetical reference been left implicit, Jong might have invoked a ritual along the lines of Max Apple's insights; but as pronounced it becomes preached and is in Gilbert Sorrentino's terms an example of telling readers what they already know (because they have just been told!). It is above all a failure attributed to valuing theme over form; and as difficult as is theme without form, the statement is destined to fall flat as fiction.

Just how flat? What in Philip Roth's work has been wildly exuberant language so appealing as to become its own subject is here, by virtue of imitating Roth on the level of theme and not technique, predictable and boring. "I envy Alexander Portnoy" (p. 161), Jong's narrator reveals. Portnoy's frankness is the choice for her mode of confession, and it is a relief to have sex handled without either hysteria or coy restraint; even the flat recounting of erotic detail can be in some cases a good effect. But when the premise of the action is built upon the statement, "What doesn't come to fucking in the end" (p. 33), fiction is reduced to an evenness that prevents any structuring leaps.

Isadora Wing, Jong's protagonist, talks about sex with few reservations or niceties. But she speaks with all the flatness of a stenographer—which the author doesn't seem to realize. "Exit husband *numero uno*" (p. 35), a line direct from sitcom television, or better yet from an old Ann Sothern script (the one where she was somebody's secretary, and office intrigues filled up the weekly half hour for season after season). Verbal stylistics are reduced to the level of "How hypocritical to go upstairs with a man you don't want to fuck, leave the one you *do* sitting there alone, and then, in a state of great excitement, fuck the one you *don't* want to fuck while pretending he's the one you do" (p. 83). Think of Ann Sothern saying that, slapping down her notebook for emphasis. For characterization it might work, but not as the voice of an entire novel. "Surrealism," Isadora says, "is my life" (p. 81), but with all sense of style removed it seems like a burning giraffe painted by David, or by Winslow Homer.

Perhaps it is the explicit Portnoy impulse that corrupts this novel and others like it. "I have told these events as plainly as possible," we read, "because nothing I say to embellish them could possibly make them more shocking" (p. 157). Jong's belief is that subject matter has not only been captured but its capture is so thrilling that presence alone will make the novel. Here is the author's reliance on the public expectation that women think like this all the time, that the stereotype of raw concupiscence is enough to sustain a work of art. Jong reveals her ultimately social realist attitude by coming out and saying that "No writer can ever tell the truth about life, namely that it is much more interesting than any book. And no writer can tell the truth about people—which is that they are much more interesting than any *characters"* (p. 201). If so, then why write novels at all, a question that *Fear of Flying* by its devotion to subject over form is unable to answer.

The real answer, of course, is that *Fear of Flying* is not read as a novel. With nothing else to distract, it is read as a "story," the same way people read Rose Kennedy's or Roxanne Pulitzer's story. That Jong seeks merely a stage for the portrayal of attitudes is evident in her sequel, *Fanny,* an eighteenth-century costume drama of a novel. But one doesn't have to give up relevance and its subsequent popularity to write something that is really fiction. The career of Anaïs Nin, for example, showed that one could be the consummate literary artist—indeed, be the very symbol of it—while making statements pertinent to the feminine sensibility. Nin, of course, waited three decades for critical tastes to catch up with her work. But today readers will create popularity for aesthetically inventive fiction, as can be seen from the works of any number of writers less hastily interested in preachment than Jong.

Judith Johnson Sherwin emerged as one of the first postmodern writers to take the role of women as a technical rather than simply topical challenge. Her stories in *The Life of Riot* (New York: Atheneum, 1970) explore how that role is a special factor in challenging the void, a void created by historical definitions of women as absence or at the very least as difference, long before all other terms were construed in terms of difference, too. Consider how she can construct a woman's monologue played against the absence of her dead husband, who is magically yet offhandedly present in such mundane places as the refrigerator, cabinet, or even garbage disposal. Only the author's projective voice can make scenes like this interesting; otherwise serving dinner and washing the dishes would be reduced to the same banality as Erica Jong's sex. Here structuring the void becomes its own substance, as happens in another story about something equally out of reach, the situation of a young Japanese wife, just deceased, whose spirit for a time haunts her husband:

> She ran and stood in front of him, holding out the fan. He stopped and stared. He looked at it. He raised his eyes and looked all around her, up and down, searching for what held the fan in the air. Almost, he saw her. Then her mind splintered in a thousand parts. She saw herself scattered throughout the world, nerves and

eyes, the heart, the hands, the spark of consciousness. Strained and trembling, she drew these fragments to her, forming a memory where there was no memory left, making words where there was no voice to speak them. The voice came from her hoarsely, in a fractured whisper. "No," it said, "You must hear. Part of me is in the ground that holds you, in the rice you eat. Part of me is in a boy plowing a field, miles away, your cousin. I am in your cousin. Part of me is before your eyes, every part of me, the conscious will that strains for you to see. I will never go. I cannot leave this place. This is my home." (p. 228)

Difference, absence, fragmentation, and unreason can be combined, in a structuring of the void, to imply a presence otherwise impossible—not a material presence, but a trace of activity no less real for its inability to be expressed as a conventional subject. Such an attitude informs Susan Quist's *Indecent Exposure* (New York: Walker, 1974) and generates an entire narrative, no part of which can be traced to any substantial provocation yet which exists with the solidity of a life as lived. Most of its action is rooted in denial. "I never meant to get married," Quist's protagonist begins. "I wanted to be famous. Actually, I wanted to be a famous writer." But obstacles to womanly presence intervene: school, marriage, and a child. Following those are other adventures, which lead to the novel at hand, making for a long but very interesting trip home. From such a narrative can there be extracted any sense of cause and effect? "Mine was a very nice family," she reasons. "When it came time for me to go to college, my family tried to pick good schools in safe areas where there was little rape. New York was definitely out. So was California. Ideally I would have gone to a women's college in the middle of the Middle West. But I was stubborn. I insisted on going east. I ended up in Pittsburgh. That was as far east as they would let me go" (p. 9).

Parental constraints on the daughter have therefore set the narrative on its present path. College itself leads to dropping out, and that in turn leads to marriage. The sixties pass by, until the protagonist drops out of marriage as well, into the counterculture, and ends up in a poorly heated walk-up in New York's East Village. "My boyfriend, who lives across the hall, has a pretty sixteen-year-old chick in his pad tonight. And he won't answer the door." Quist's narrator then considers the pattern of her life, the plan of any confessional novel, but lodges responsibility for it in an interesting place. "Do you suppose it's all because they let me go to that lousy school? I don't know" (p. 11).

It is this freshness, lack of inhibition, and refusal of dead seriousness that makes *Indecent Exposure* such a good narrative. But the basis for all those qualities is in Quist's talent for making the conditions of her identity, based as they are in absence and difference, generate the story as a structuring device—a device that structures the utter void of what her life would be according to reasonable (or, perhaps "male") terms. Because of this, the past itself is never dully repeated, demanding the enhancement of a spicey Portnoyish vulgarity to maintain interest. Instead the narrator keeps herself and the reader in a continual present, emphasizing the act of structuring rather than what is structured, carefully examining the past only according to how she is now (Jong's contrary device had been to enhance Isadora Wing's present identity with the salaciousness of her past and her boldness in speaking so frankly about it, an example of structure surrendering to subject matter). In the protagonist's own novel she makes films with the same vital sense found in the story itself. "It was physical, like dancing," she recounts. "I had to move around to get my shot. I liked the way I could be standing a block away from someone, but with the camera, I could look into his eyes like they were right in front of me. I could fill the lens, the screen, a whole wall with just a caterpillar" (p. 96). Only the finest fiction has this quality, built as it is on the act of structuring (in this case making a film) rather than expounding thematics (the subject, after all, is in the bleak and unrewarding East Village). As for her parents' worry that attending college in the high-rape density of the east would lead to a life of ruin, Quist's protagonist, having faced the vacuity of subject matter, can ask herself "Which dangers are real?" and answer, with great structural capability, "All of them. Or none. Probability has nothing to do with it. You can guard against all, one, some, none. In the end it's all the same" (p. 151).

Susan Quist's work shows not only that the confessional novel needs all the structural techniques of fiction, but that the best part about describing sex is using one's imagination to do it. Like death, the ultimately unverifiable personal experience, sex is a subject that defies any certainty of representation. In trying to capture its essence, one learns that what exists is not so much sex as a structure of ideas about it existing in the space "sex" would occupy. Imagine a net as extensive as all human history and that net being cast out to recover just what sex is. Yet the subject escapes, and what remains is just the net itself. And the nature of this net is what determines the quality of one's effort. In *Fear of Flying* the net has been formed by snide associations with the more vulgar aspects of the act. What do we talk about when we talk about sex? In Jong's case it can be excrement. In Quist's novel, even though there is just as much candor, there is never an attempt to make that candor into a fetish for the unreachable subject; instead, readers see the author's structuring as encompassing the full range of human interests and emotions, with the narrative's whole being brought to bear on the action of a sexual life. Here is the long root of experience, rather than the hasty, salacious quip, that makes all the difference for valid art.

Standing at the forefront of writers who use the constraint of gender not as a sociological topic but as a generative force for their narratives is Grace Paley, and her *Enormous Changes at the Last Minute* (New York: Farrar, Straus & Giroux, 1974), as revealed in its remarkable disclaimer crediting something as real as the book itself: "*Everyone in this book is imagined into life except the father. No matter what story he has to live in, he's my father, I. Goodside, M.D., artist, and story teller.*" Signed with Paley's initials, her statement reveals a noble constraint: of gender, parenthood, and generational difference all combined to place her writing in a special position, not the least of which involves the real presence of her father amid whatever else she may construe. Near the collection's end he appears in an influential role, as Paley takes the occasion of "A Conversation with My Father" to let him have his say about her narrative art, hectoring her as a man born in and formed by the nineteenth century who requires that his daughter's fiction have the force and resolution of Tolstoy and Dostoevsky. But even before this face-off of contradictory methods, Paley has shaped many of her stories from the point of view of a mother or a daughter and, against all fatherly imperatives to resolve and conclude (and therefore to judge) the fates of her characters, maintains a more open-ended style of narrative—a style in which the act of structuring is more interesting, sensible, and rewarding than any attempt to resolve things as a subject.

Can there indeed be such a thing as a woman's perspective on such structuring? As a beginning, one can listen to these tales with an ear for voice, as in many of Grace Paley's stories the vocal quality of the narrative carries with it qualities associated with the womanly rather than with the male—not because of subject matter but due to the way this voice tells the story, the way it structures the material. Consider the painfully brief story "Samuel," whose four pages expand to encompass not just the horror of a child's death but its lifetime consequences for others.

"Some boys are very tough" (p. 103), the story begins, a plain statement of just five words from which all else will unfold, contained within that statement as it is. Being tough, they fear nothing; and by fearing nothing they lead themselves into risky situations: on the roof, in the cellar, and between moving cars on the subway. Of these possibilities, Paley chooses the third, and starts the second paragraph with another short, direct sentence, indicating that four such boys are out there jiggling on the swaying platform. They are being watched, but in different ways, as the older male passengers amusedly think back to their own adolescent adventures while the women become angry at the spectacle. Some knit their brows together, assuming their frowns will stop this dangerous behavior. One wants to intervene, but fears the boys will laugh at and embarrass her. Another frets that the boys' mothers don't know' where they are. But they do, the story tells us: "Their mothers all knew that they had gone to see the missile exhibit on Fourteenth Street" (p. 104).

Here is one of the few signals of attitude not contained within the generative power of language alone. From that first sentence Paley has been careful to make each subsequent line develop from something potential in the one previous, much as a linguist can develop a universe of statements from the most rudimentary beginning structure. But the reference to missiles stands out: a phallic symbol, of course, but more immediately a reference to male aggression and boyish fascination with such things. Though referential rather than interactive, it still fits within the system of male-female differences that Paley's narrative has established among the passengers' reactions to the boys.

It is at this point that the woman who had held back for fear of embarrassment asserts herself, recalling her own boy at home and determining to prevent trouble here. Opening the door, warning the boys to sit down, and threatening to call the conductor if they don't, she finds her intervention to be momentarily successful. But then two of the boys begin teasing the two others for submitting, and a round of dangerous roughhousing begins as the group begin pounding each other on the back. Has the woman actually made things worse? In the story's turning point, Paley reminds her readers that only a characteristically masculine act can do that, taking the woman's care and caution and transforming it all into something tragic. As the boys' behavior becomes disconcerting to all in the car, a passenger finally acts, but for all the wrong reasons and with a fatal result: "One of the men whose boyhood had been more watchful than brave became angry. He stood up straight and looked at the boys for a couple of seconds. Then he walked in a citizenly way to the end of the car, where he pulled the emergency cord. Almost at once, with a terrible hiss, the pressure of air abandoned the brakes and the wheels were caught and held" (p. 105). Note the reason for acting—anger, not care—and the adverb used to describe his action: *citizenly*. Concerned less for the boys than for himself, the man has invoked authority and acted in a critically judgmental manner, the effect of which is not only humanly destructive but patently unjust. As the car screeches to a halt everyone is thrown about, including one of the boys who falls to his death.

The death happens in a flash, taking just sixteen short words. What follows, however, is an enormity of action bursting forth in implication from the story's remaining half page. There is silence, followed by the grim business of an experienced trainman who removes the body. As a clue to what will happen, some of the women wonder if Samuel, who hasn't been identified by name or habits until a moment before his death, might be an only child. Yet there have been no cries, no screams, no outbursts of grief. These wait until the second to last paragraph, where a policeman is sent to tell Samuel's mother. Then the scream begins—reserved for the one whose loss is greatest—and continues without abatement into the chartless future, where even after bearing another child the mother is left with her loss unfulfilled. "She and her husband together have had other children," the piece concludes, "but never again will a boy exactly like Samuel be known" (p. 106).

By locating her story's conclusion squarely within the mother's grief, Paley indicates the structural truth about the void of death; the scream so obvious from the narrative's first line and struggling for expression in every act thereafter is finally given voice where it is most deeply felt. Although many others contribute to the structuring, no act is complete until the mother's voice is heard. And that voice itself is not the articulation of a subject but the expression of the void her child's death has made. All else, the reader must acknowledge, has been inadequate signaling, including some, such as fear of embarrassment and citizenly ire, that have helped create the void itself. And behind it all lies the system of male-female difference that sets the track for Paley's narrative.

When constraints of gender figure thematically as well, the structure of Paley's art is all the more emphatic. In "The Burdened Man" the interest lies in just how obsessive the male's role as provider can be, to the point of fretting as electricity is consumed (hallway lights left on), gas is burned up (as his wife bakes rolls in the expensive medium), and long-distance phone calls are "immediately clicked into the apparatus of AT&T and added against him by IBM" (p. 109). It seems like a conspiracy, especially when he, his wife, and his son each buy a copy of the day's newspaper. All of these expenses, of course, are minimal— mere pennies. Yet it is the fact that pennies add up that so infuriates him, and when in making good a neighbor's loss for which he is responsible is faced with being given two cents in change he can bear no more, flying into a rage and precipitating a call to the police. Yet even here there is a pedestrian little system that resolves things without ever having to deal with the thing in itself: "The police arrive at once from somewhere and are disgusted to see two grown-up people throwing money at each other and crying. But the neighborhood is full of shade trees and pretty lawns. The police forgive them and watch them go home in the same direction (because they're next-door neighbors)" (p. 110).

By a similar system of correspondences the two become friendly to the point of anticipated passion: "they have coffee at her house and explain everything. They each tell one story about when they were young" (p. 111). As with the lawns and shade trees that provide a schedule of judgment for the police, these single stories each serve as a bond from which a romance might well develop. But the neighbor's husband intervenes before anything can happen, barging into one of their Sunday meetings enraged, drunk, and armed. Does he kill his wife and her presumed lover? No—for Grace Paley that would be an inappropriately direct resolution, far too neat for the world of systems based on such oddities as individual kilograms of electricity, cubic feet of gas, and nickels for the daily paper, all of which have conspired to burden her hapless hero. As the husband opens up with his .45, the spray of bullets takes in its own field of targets: "he shot and shot, the man, the woman, the wall, the picture window, the coffee pot," and eventually himself, in the foot. As the newspaper tells it, "Sgt. Armand

Kielly put an end today to his wife's alleged romance with neighbor
Alfred Ciaro by shooting up his kitchen, Mr. Kielly, himself, and his
career" (p. 114). Like a Gertrude Stein sentence or a Jorge Luis Borges
list of categorizations, Paley's system is so intellectually unrelated as to
deconstruct itself. But such is her subject: disorganized and anti-
hierarchical, yet pertinent to the story's life as lived. As a subject it may
be chaotic, but as a system it pertains to what has happened without
letting presuppositions about the nature of experience overrule.

Paley's understanding of gender extends to the male form of structuring as well. In "The Little Girl," the collection's most violent story,
she gives the narrator's role to a male, not simply for the benefit of his
perception but so that the narrative's action can take place within his
own adjustment of attitude. Such a portrayal is accomplished by
technique rather than by theme alone, especially in the way the character's voice structures his world. From the second word of the story's
first line we know the narrator is a black, urban American relatively
low on the socioeconomic and educational scale: "Carter stop by the
café early" (p. 151). From this characterizing speech all else follows,
including the plot—which involves Carter borrowing the man's room
for sex with a fourteen-year-old girl—but also the action as it transpires in the narrator's mind. It becomes his task not just to describe
Carter's acts but to react to them and then make a judgment, in the
process transforming his own beliefs and standards.

The narrator's change is subtle. That he is impending toward one is
evident from the way Paley positions him: outside the act of seduction
and ravagement but still involved (it is his room, after all), critical of
Carter—recalling that his own method of picking up young girls was
more cautious—yet complicit by gender and past practice. One sees
why Paley chose a male rather than female voice, for its tone cannot be
immediately judgmental, but is instead one that remains curious about
the events portrayed.

As for the little girl of the title, her role is shown in language before
any thematic action takes place, with the risk of her being in such a
place encoded in the adolescent vulnerability of her speech: "I just left
for good. My mother don't let me do a thing. I got to do the breakfast
dishes when I get home from school and clean and do my two brothers'
room and they don't have to do nothing. And I got to be home in my
room by 10 p.m. weekdays and 12 p.m. just when the fun starts
Saturday and nothing is going on in that town. Nothing! It's dead, a

sleeping hollow. *And the prejudice, whew!"* (p. 152). Rather than giving the reader signals from which attitudes can be assumed, Paley provides a system of structuring the world from which much more about the little girl can be deduced, for we are seeing her mind in action. Grammar and usage alone deconstruct the frivolity of her complaint: her mother won't let her "do" anything but makes her "do" all the work; she is forced to be home early (by her standards) and thus miss the action in a town where there is none (except prejudice, which she notes in ofay camaraderie scarcely less awkward than her previous posturings). She is no match for the smooth-talking Carter, whom the narrator can mimic as well: "He says, I got a nice place, you could just relax and rest and decide what to do next. Take a shower. Whatever you like. Anyways you do is O.K. My, you are sweet. You better'n Miss America. How old you say you was?" (p. 153).

When the sex comes, it is vicious, brutal, and direct, leading to the little girl's destruction. In pathological detail the narrator recounts her ripped and broken parts, and shudders at the fact that in the end her body was dumped from the window of his fifth-floor room. With this the story's overt action ends, but the narrator remains to puzzle out its implications. He begins within character, simply trying to be practical. "But wasn't it a shame, them two studs," he complains. "Why they take it out on her? After so many fluffy little chicks. They could of played her easy. Why Carter seen it many times hisself. She could of stayed the summer" (p. 157). From here he tries to distance himself, but can't—it was his room where the outrage took place. And then the personal nature of the little girl's suffering hits him, beginning with the incanted statement, "I don't stop thinking, That child . . . That child." And from here it "comes" to him, an explanation for all that happened—not as observed action and not even by propounding Carter's point of view, but by imagining himself within the little girl's system of understanding, which means by imagining himself across the constraint of gender and as the little girl himself. This passage would conclude the story, except for the four-word paragraph that ends, the only words in the piece that are not the character's own:

> And it come to me yesterday, I lay down after work: Maybe it wasn't no one [who threw her to her death]. Maybe she pull herself the way she was, she must of thought she was gutted inside her skin. She must of been in a horror what she got to remem-

ber—what her folks would see. Her life look to be disgusting like a squashed fish, so what she did: she made up some power somehow and raise herself up that windowsill and hook herself onto it and then what I see, she just topple herself out. That what I think right now.

That is what happened. (pp. 157–58)

Throughout the story all of Paley's points have been made through voice, specifically voice that by its structuring habits reveals the character and his or her posture toward the world. In the penultimate paragraph we once again have an individual's systematic approach and can follow what is worked out from it. Then, to end things with the author's authority, we hear a voice not previously used, a voice whose grammatical correctness ("That is what happened" rather than the characteristic "That what happened") seals the narrator's statement as what the author herself believes. And all of it comes from structuring the void rather than seeking to portray it as a subject.

Rarely does a Grace Paley story rely on feminine narrative alone, for a key effect comes from seeing the difference between male and female structures. "A Conversation with My Father" uses this contrast to articulate the special nature of Paley's work, which existing as it does within the literary tradition must engage and debate the masculine point of view. In this story the male role is classically paternal: the narrator wants stories written within a systematics that is nineteenth-century, Russian, and male—his own, in other words, though he cannot see it that way, because in asking for judgment, resolution, and closure he is merely seeking a world construed after his own axioms. Paley's narrator, however, as a writer of stories lives within an entirely different system. For her, plot is not something that satisfies but is rather that "absolute line between two points, which I've always despised. Not for literary reasons, but because it takes all hope away. Everyone, real or invented, deserves the open destiny of life" (p. 162).

Yet to please him, she proposes a story that resolves itself. The problem is, it only runs one paragraph, so enclosing does its author find the nature of plot. Chided that she has misunderstood him on purpose, she tries again, this time yielding a full-length narrative much like those Paley herself has published. When he seems pleased with its finality, however, she objects; even with its authorship completed, the story remains alive (and open to interpretation) with its readers, and as a reader she can object that the ending "doesn't have to be" (p. 166). Why? Because beyond all constraints of authorship and readership she is still a person, one whose principles refuse to "leave her there in that house crying" as the story would have it. Now her father's objections are the most serious, challenging her view of tragedy. "When will you look it in the face?" he asks (p. 167), and the piece ends without her answer—because, given what the reader has seen, Paley's narrator cannot, for doing so would be to admit that age and a failing heart—two of the most inexorable plot devices imaginable, if one were to believe in plot—will soon rob her of her father.

In her volume's concluding and by far longest story, "The Long Distance Runner," Paley's narrator exposes herself to just such conflicting plot lines of experience, in this case the lines that run back into her past and have remained buried for over a generation. Middle-aged, divorced, and the mother of two teenaged children, she wonders how her life has been structured to arrive at this point, and undertakes to retrace its experience to the roots, taking her back to her childhood apartment where now another woman lives with her family, herself structuring an existence. In terms of subject matter that existence is as different from Paley's narrator as can be. Racially the difference is between black and white; culturally the gap is almost beyond language's ability to bridge, and the new economic reality of postmodern America makes the contrast a bitter one, the poverty of the narrator's earlier twentieth-century urban neighborhood utterly uncomparable to the desolation being suffered now in what has become a black ghetto. Nor can the minority experience be the same, Jewish-American carrying far different connotations and denotations than being African-American. Yet when the focus shifts from the subject of experience itself to the act of structuring it, the two women's narratives are suddenly quite similar.

"The Long Distance Runner" begins with a metaphor: running, as exercise, has no goal other than itself—no points to amass or opponent to beat, just its own activity as a process to experience. The narrator confesses that her goal is, in terms of substance, pointless: to go "round and round the county from the sea side to the bridges, along the old neighborhood streets a couple of times, before old age and urban renewal ended them and me" (p. 179). This act involves setting aside a certain amount of her present, especially as devoted to the goals of raising children and tending a family:

Then summer came, my legs seemed strong. I kissed the kids goodbye. They were quite old by then. It was near the time for parting anyway. I told Mrs. Raftery to look in now and then and give them some of that rotten Celtic supper she makes.

I told them they could take off any time they wanted to. Go lead your private life, I said. Only leave me out of it. (p. 180)

On a lark she jogs into the neighborhood of her distant childhood— and suddenly finds herself surrounded by a crowd of unsympathetic black people: "Who you?" "Who that?" "Look at her! Just look! When you seen a fatter ass?" (p. 181). Their verbal hostility, however, is transformable by a textuality of the narrator's own. She recalls that her people had their own way of speech and their own sense of place. On these levels she begins to make contact. But the strongest bond is forged by the most unlikely of textual structures, here in their virtually bombed out ghetto neighborhood. How many flowers' names do you know, she asks some of the children, and a young girl—who now lives in the same building the woman once occupied—names several, using her Girl Scout publication, *A Handbook of Wild Flowers.*

This structuring of the void—wild flowers in the South Bronx—is the vehicle by which the otherwise alien parties connect. Merely having lived here forty years before, or having her own family at home now, is not enough; indeed, the young girl is frightened by the story-teller's reference to her boys at home. But their mutual citation of flowers gets her in the door, as it were; and once in, as the guest of the old apartment's new tenant, Mrs. Luddy, the narrator can settle in for an incredible three week stay and a very credible experience in how women structure the void of existence:

> The living room was something like ours, only we had less plastic. There may have been less plastic in the world at that time. Also, my mother had set beautiful cushions everywhere, on beds and chairs. It was the way she expressed herself, artistically, to em-broider at night or take strips of flowered cotton and sew them across ordinary white or blue muslin in the most delicate designs, the way women have always used materials that live and die in hunks and tatters to say: This is my place.
>
> Mrs. Luddy said, Uh huh!
>
> Of course, I said, men don't have that outlet. That's how come they run around so much.

Till they drunk enough to lay down, she said.

Yes, I said, on a large scale you can see it in the world. First they make something, then they murder it. Then they write a book about how interesting it is.

You got something there, she said. Sometimes she said, Girl, you don't know *nothing*. (p. 189)

Like her running, the storyteller's experience in Mrs. Luddy's household is without specific goal or even duration; one day her host simply says it's time to leave and back she jogs to her family. They wonder where she's been but are unable to comprehend her story. She repeats it. They say, "What?" And so the narrator repeats it for us, a single paragraph's distillation of the twenty pages preceding, taking the compressed form used in earlier short stories devoted to discussing and debating fiction with her father: "Because it isn't usually so simple. Have you known it to happen much nowadays? A woman inside the steamy energy of middle age runs and runs. She finds the houses and streets where her childhood happened. She lives in them. She learns as though she was still a child what in the world is coming next" (p. 198).

Why doesn't the narrator's family understand? Because they've been given plot alone, the story in terms of its subject rather than technique. We as readers, however, can appreciate the experience, for we have seen it as a structuring exercise, to which this summary now serves less as a conclusion than as coda.

Grace Paley's stories in *Enormous Changes at the Last Minute* are less about things than they *are* things: undertakings in the structuring of voids. And whether those voids be the unspeakable factors of a child's death, a neighbor's encounter with violence, the rape and murder of a barely adolescent girl, or a late middle-aged woman wondering how she got where she is, Paley's narratives give a solid sense not of those voids themselves but rather the experience of them.

6

Constraint:

Vietnam

As with gender, the constraint of warfare as a structure for action demands that the narrator proceed by indirection. That such practice was followed by the war's principal narrator and generative force is apparent from how President Lyndon B. Johnson spoke about it. "This country's domestic policy is a direct reflection of its foreign policy," he was fond of saying. "If people want to know what we are doing abroad, they should take a close look at what we are doing at home." Johnson's statement was quickly textualized as a structure for understanding American involvement in Vietnam and was published by the antiwar movement as part of an especially graphic poster: a close-up news photo of the Madison Police Department's tactical squad clubbing a group of students who had sat down in front of the University of Wisconsin's Commerce Building to protest the Dow Chemical recruiting taking place inside. The spatial juxtaposition of words and picture was instructive, for here indeed was a virtual identity between domestic and foreign policy, an act of structuring that clarified matters far better than any attempt to articulate the void itself that Vietnam had become for us.

An equally instructive parallel can be drawn between domestic novels and stories and Vietnam war fiction of the same era: that if one wanted to know what was going on in fiction about the war, it might be best to take a close look at how fiction was being written at home. True, the subject matter of these two realms of writing could be quite different, with Ronald Sukenick and Richard Brautigan interested in such things as the metaphoric decline of the novel and the new pervasiveness of such bizarre things as "trout wine" and "watermelon sugar," while William Pelfry was sending his infantry out into the field and Josiah Bunting was running down the command structure of the army to show how actions undertaken at the level of division determine the life of an individual soldier walking point on patrol. Of course, this same age had demonstrated philosophically that subject itself was a chimera, that all that really existed was a system of differences employed in structuring that void. Yet among the writers at home a similar indirection was being followed, using postmodern techniques for a war nearly a quarter-century past. Joseph Heller had begun the decade of the 1960s with *Catch-22*, treating not the emerging struggle in Southeast Asia but World War II in the Mediterranean and southern Italy, while Kurt Vonnegut had ended the decade with an even more Vietnamized novel, yet not about Vietnam—although the protagonist's son becomes a Green Beret serving there, the novel's war scenes are limited to Belgium, Luxembourg, and Germany in late 1944 and early 1945. With the new skepticism of subject matter the times provided, we now know that both Heller's and Vonnegut's books were as much about Vietnam as they were about the European theater two decades before. Why so? Because of their structurally disruptive form, the first aesthetic lesson from the 1960s. It is at this point that the better Vietnam war novels and domestic experiments coincide.

There is, however, a third element to consider for text and context to be complete: not just what was taking place abroad, and not just what was going on at home, but what was happening to the principles of fiction itself. Ronald Sukenick, for example, was running down the list of components in traditional narrative and finding that each of them, from character and consequence to time and reality themselves, no longer existed in the philosophic world that must underlie any stance for fiction. Even if authors would attempt to write from a conventional viewpoint, their works could no longer be read strictly representationally, for William H. Gass had made the case for fiction being not an assemblage of things but of words, while Gilbert Sorrentino had shown how the shorthand use of signs for social attitudes allowed the writer to slip out from under the obligations of his or her art. Nor were these positions being taken in a critical vacuum, for thinking had passed from its positivistic and existential modes, both of which enhanced fiction's role for thematic spokesmanship, and adopted a new posture of critical self-examination, expressed most accessibly in the works of Roland Barthes which sold to popular readers in France and were being translated in England and the United States.

Looking around one could see in October 1966 that 150,000 American military personnel were stationed in Vietnam, where President Johnson paid a secret visit to urge them on. During that same month Donald Barthelme corrected galley proof for his first novel, *Snow White,* while the *New Yorker* was having its readership reeducated to the fictional complexities of such Barthelme stories as "The Falling Dog" and "Kierkegaard Unfair to Schlegel"; in Haight-Ashbury, Richard Brautigan was preparing another part of the culture for his just-completed *Trout Fishing in America*; and Kurt Vonnegut, who had struggled in academic and commercial obscurity for nearly twenty years, was just now taking the first steps toward being embraced as the era's great public writer. And also in that coincidental month of October 1966 Johns Hopkins University hosted an international conference entitled *The Languages of Criticism and the Sciences of Man* (Baltimore: Johns Hopkins University Press, 1970, edited by Richard Macksey and Eugene Donato), bringing Roland Barthes, Jacques Derrida, and a host of other Continental thinkers to the United States for the first major forum on their work.

Consider the common turning point for all three concerns. By late 1966 the Vietnam experience could be described as one of uncertainty in the face of disrupted forms and as yet unanswered questions: why was this war neither fightable nor supportable in conventional terms? In fiction similar traditional certainties of order, coherence, and authority were being unsettled by writers who declined to accept the realistic novel's great tradition of linear time, physical space, and God-like moral stature. And at Johns Hopkins, Barthes and Derrida were asking similar questions about communication itself—specifically, about the gap between the world and our words for it. Could the term "to write" be reconstrued as an intransitive verb? And if so, what would happen to our literature? Could it have no center of authority at all, meaning that everything would become not truth but just endless discussions of what truth might be—and never pretending for a minute to find it?

There are complex terms for all of this, which Barthes and Derrida brought with them and which, to Anglo-American ears, have confused the tone of what should in fact be a clarion call. "When everything became a system where the central signified, the original or transcendental signified, is never absolutely present outside a system of differences," Derrida said, then "everything became discourse." A transcendental signified is simply an artificial but commonly agreed upon identification which by virtue of long use becomes accepted as natural fact. "The absence of the transcendental signified," Derrida continued, anticipating the overthrow of conventional values taking place all around him in this America of October 1966, "extends the domain and the interplay of signification *ad infinitum*" (p. 249), an apt description of the alleged dialogue taking place in our country during these years as the social fabric was rent and hundreds of thousands of soldiers and civilians perished in Vietnam.

At the same conference Barthes was more direct, trusting only that his audience would know that fifty years before Ferdinand de Saussure had suggested that the practices of linguistics might bear application to the culture's larger discourse among itself—in other words that there might be a discipline of semiotics, the study of how signs function in society. Admit that writing is a system of signs and it is not hard to appreciate how such cultural signs (which we insist on calling "facts") are always double, referring us to something else but also to themselves. Identifying the particulars of this double reference could be revealing indeed. In 1966 the United States was fighting in Vietnam; but a decade before, Barthes and Derrida had seen their respective native lands at war in Algeria. For the popular press in 1955 Barthes had written two important essays later collected and combined as "African Grammar" in *The Eiffel Tower and Other Mythologies* (New York: Hill & Wang, 1979), expressing a view he could have easily transposed to the language of America in Vietnam. The lessons were certainly the same: that the "official vocabulary of African affairs is, as we might suspect, purely axiomatic. Which is to say that it has no value as communication, but only as intimidation. It therefore constitutes a *writing,* i.e., a language intended to bring about a coincidence between norms and facts, and to give a cynical reality the guarantee of a noble morality" (p. 103).

As we might expect of Barthes, he went on to establish how the language France used to describe the Algerian War of Independence functions as a code—and by code, he meant a system in which words have no viable relation to their content other than an occasional contrary one (such as "pacification," a term used again by politicians and the military in Vietnam). For the skeptic of language there could be a certain amount of decoding (the lofty and imposing "destiny" for French intentions, the derogatory and diminutive "band" for any group resisting those intentions), but such piecemeal redefinitions (in the tradition of ragpicking, which shares the same etymology as the French word *défricher,* "to decode") take us no farther than such old chestnuts as Orwell's "Politics and the English Language" and any sixties peace activist's phrasebook for the Johnson administration's lexicon of distortion. More important than correcting an individual word was understanding the principle of grammar at work in its selection: using a word as an algebraic symbol so that it might have "an indeterminate value of signification, in itself without meaning and therefore capable of receiving any meaning, whose function is to fill a gap between signifier and signified" (p. 104). One such word is *honor,* which both the French and the Americans used to describe their intentions. But there is much more at stake than the word. As Barthes said in 1955, "*Honor* is quite specifically our *mana,* something like a blank page in which we arrange the entire collection of inadmissible meanings and which we make sacred in the manner of a taboo" (p. 104). Barthes' work, which has facilitated our understanding of the American 1960s as helpfully as has the commentary of any stateside critic, expands from simple linguistics to matters that are political, sociological, and ultimately anthropological. At the root of his anthropology is the admission that in postmodern times certain modes of discourse no longer apply.

Europeans have helped us this way before, pointing out that some problems remain inexplicable only because our traditional ways of understanding have become inadequate. How do you talk about Auschwitz, Theodor Adorno asks, when the entire genre of Hegelian speculative discourse is swallowed up in its abyss? Auschwitz has simply invalidated the presupposition of that discourse, the belief that reality and rationality are interchangeable terms. How do you talk about the Hungarian Revolution of 1956, Albert Camus asks, when the entire genre of historical materialist discourse disintegrated when it became apparent that no one, not even the Russians, any longer believed that communism and the proletariat were interchangeable terms? How do you talk about the events of 1968—whether they be in Prague, in Paris, or climaxing in Chicago—when the entire genres of democratic discourse and republican dialogue are clubbed senseless by the state's police? From then on the belief that valid concerns of the community can be discussed within the forms of parliamentary representation is a dead one. And what about the traditional novel, with its comforting

allusions that the individual is the significant focus among the phenomena of reality (characterization), that linear time is the reigning
form of duration for consciousness (historical narration), that reality
itself can be located by empirical observation (description), the convic-
tion that the world is logical and comprehensible (causal sequence),
and most of all the belief that the world is predictable, not mysterious,
and answerable to the writer's control? These questions about the
lapsed premises for fiction are drawn from Ronald Sukenick's *In Form:
Digressions on the Act of Fiction* (Carbondale: Southern Illinois University Press, 1985, pp. 3–4), and are in fact a development of his own
fiction as first undertaken in *The Death of the Novel and Other Stories*
(New York: Dial Press, 1969, pp. 41–42 especially). But Sukenick's
assessment is one shared by European critics and mirrored by our own
sixties revolution in fiction, a transformation just now beginning to
have a permanent effect on mainstream work. Perhaps in 1995, when
probabilities imply that the United States may be involved in a major
land war somewhere, Sukenick will write a novel about Vietnam, just
as Heller and Vonnegut had to wait until the Vietnam War was underway before completing their own books about World War II. The
lesson is that one cannot talk about an experience until the discourse
that experience invalidates is cleared out of the way and replaced by a
style of communication pertinent to the matter at hand. In the fiction of
the Vietnam War we witness a struggle to find such words and forms.

To understand the impact of the Vietnam War on American culture
and its fictions, one must take a close look at the structural challenges
to three things: the military strategists' planning and their tacticians'
conduct, the fiction writers' remarkably similar struggles with form,
and the cultural theorists' explanations for what was happening—for
what was fated to happen, if one heeds the French experience at Dien
Bien Phu (where their ambitions for Vietnam met final defeat), at
the Ecole Normale Supérieure (where Derrida was teaching), and
the Centre National de Recherche Scientifique (where Barthes first
worked). Military conduct is the most obvious topic, and American
novelists were quick to draw on its troubles for their form. When the
journalist David Halberstam tried his hand at a Vietnam novel, *One
Very Hot Day* (Boston: Houghton Mifflin, 1967), he found certain
structural choices to be almost mandatory. How could he capture the
war's experience, which had yet to reach its high point of action? Boil
it down to the events of just one day. How could he codify its politics?

Have an American adviser accompany a South Vietnamese patrol, and let him wonder about his role and theirs. Make him a World War II vet, so he can make explicit comments on the radical change in tactics, and allow plenty of thinking time on this long patrol, so that strategy itself can become a thoroughly incomprehensible problem:

> We didn't know how simple it was, and how good we had it. Sure we walked, but in a straight line. Boom, Normandy beaches, and then you set off for Paris and Berlin. Just like that. No retracing, no goddam circles, just straight ahead. All you needed was a compass and good sense. But here you walk in a goddam circle, and then you go home, and then you go out the next day and wade through a circle, and then you go home and the next day you go out and reverse the circle you did the day before, erasing it. Every day the circles get bigger and emptier. Walk them one day, erase them the next. In France you always knew where you were, how far you had walked, and how far you had to go. But in this goddam place, Christ, if I knew how far I had walked, it would break my heart. From Normandy to Berlin and back, probably.
> (p. 79)

In this passage all three areas of interest converge: military tactics, fictive form, and even deconstructionist thought. Halberstam's character, Captain Beaupré, is facing the same trackless jungle as do André Malraux's protagonist and antagonist in the first major Western novel about the Vietnam experience, *The Royal Way* (New York: Harrison Smith and Robert Haas, 1935, translated by Stuart Gilbert from *La Voie Royale*, Paris, 1930). In such an amorphous, primeval place, Malraux asks "Here what act of man had any meaning, what human will but spent its staying power?" (p. 101). Malraux's characters, like Captain Beaupré (French for "bowsprit," the leading edge of a ship), make an incursion into a strange new realm which resists their traditional principles of organization. They try to structure it, but in fact they are structuring a void. Beaupré knows for sure that his Vietnam experience is nothing like World War II, where America invaded the Continent and rearranged its national and political boundaries in just another occidental form—which is exactly the style of Western progress the military reality of Vietnam would disallow. To Beaupré it doesn't seem real; his tour of duty is not for the duration, but for 365 days, an imposition of time and space he finds distressing: "He wished the troops would go faster, would move it out, and he wished he were a real officer, someone who could give commands and then see them obeyed, who could send a patrol here and another there, could make the troops go fast, go slow, be brave, be strong; wished to be hated, to be feared, even to be loved, but to be an officer and in charge" (p. 155). But as the paragraph implies, the grammar of this new war will not allow it—the syntactic mode is intransitive, not transitive, with no real structure other than an unending series of "ands." Make a circle, then erase it, leaving no sense of presence other than Derrida's trace—an erasure if there ever was one, for the circles only get emptier as they grow. "In France you always knew where you were," as Derrida might have told Halberstam in 1966 as he wrote this book; but here in Vietnam he and his character will have to figure it out for themselves. And for now all Captain Beaupré can do is punctuate this trackless grammar with a series of "goddams."

In time American soldiers and their novelist-creators will walk away from the experience, like Tim O'Brien's Cacciato. And notice where Cacciato's pursuers walk: to the same safe haven America's prototypical war novelist, Ernest Hemingway, found just up the hill from Barthes's eventual professorship at the Collège de France. But what's more interesting is how, in certain hands, fictive form itself adopts the thematics of Halberstam and the philosophical theory of Derrida to make the novel more properly responsive to the transformative experience of Vietnam. With *One Very Hot Day* American writers begin the search for structure common to the best of subsequent Vietnam novels: how to organize this war that defies all previous military, political, and even fictive patterns. The novelist starts with basics, a single day's patrol, but on it his World War II veteran (here a captain, but in most other books a career sergeant) loses all sense of purpose and achievement, frustrating the author as his character is frustrated himself by this experience of Vietnam that makes little conventional sense.

Whether experienced by a journalist on a Guggenheim like Halberstam or by a literate soldier on patrol like William Pelfrey, Vietnam proved to be a war unlike any other American writers had confronted. Tom Mayer, a representative of the first group, writes about such difficulties in his collection of short stories, *The Weary Falcon* (Boston: Houghton Mifflin, 1971), which includes the situation of "the US Marines landing at Chu Lai where the troops came storming out of the amtracks and up the beach like John Wayne in *The Sands of Iwo Jima* only to find twenty photographers on the top of the first dune taking pictures of it all" (p. 95). In similar terms Pelfrey's *The Big V* (New York: Liveright, 1972) fails as a realistic combat novel despite its author's credentials as a veteran infantryman because the war his narrator experiences is measured constantly against its familiar images on television (pictures sent back by the first group) and in the movies (images created by still older writers), and therefore it never has the chance to escape the tired pop-art clichés assigned to every act. "I fired one round on semi-automatic," we read. "His body jerked erect, almost like a gangster blown back by a sawed-off shotgun, only screaming, hoarse, with his mouth gaping; more like an Indian, his arms flying up and dropping the rifle" (p. 36). Pelfrey's narrator can find no vocabulary for the war beyond such trite images because his vision is allowed to extend no farther than the video adventures of his youth— and even he must flip through this encyclopedia of signs, from gangster movies to cowboy-and-Indian shoot-'em-ups, to find the right mode of description. That Vietnam was fought on such a level is less frightening than the thought that the war was comprehended this way by some artists searching for a form of understanding. The virtue of Pelfrey's novel is that it at least recognizes that signs are signs and that some of those signs may be lies—a conclusion Donald Barthelme's almost thoroughly domestic fiction was reaching back home. In Robin Moore's *The Green Berets* (1965) and John Briley's *The Traitors* (1969), however, there is no such self-awareness of the systems of constraint within which the writer labors. And unlike Kurt Vonnegut's promise to Mary O'Hare in the first chapter of *Slaughterhouse-Five,* Moore and Briley have indeed written war books in which there *are* roles for John Wayne, Frank Sinatra, and whoever else looks good in central casting's battle fatigues.

Outstripping the politics and military theories of earlier wars and older generations, the truth of Vietnam became a test of the artist's imagination—a test Moore and Briley would fail, but which others would pass and, in the process of doing so, join the aesthetic revolution taking place among fiction writers at home. Three of the best novels about the war while it was still being fought were written by authors who were never there as active participants and who removed the action of their books to broader perspective. In *The Prisoners of Quai Dong* (1967) Victor Kolpacoff suggests the sense of Vietnam by writing about a military jail where the order of life has all the tedium, uncertainty, and senselessness of the war going on outside—particularly when the narrator, on charge for refusing duty, is asked to participate in the interrogation by torture of a Viet Cong suspect. William Eastlake's *The Bamboo Bed* (1969) finds an even more appropriate perspective on this surreal war: over the jungle combat, above even the monsoon engulfing the action, in a rescue helicopter used for in-flight trysts between a postmodern Captain Tarzan and Nurse Jane. The ship is more noted for people it has not rescued, including an infantry company led by its captain into a ritualistic recreation of Custer's Last Stand, with the Viet Cong as obliging Indians (a recataloging of Pelfrey's collection of signs and symbols now more responsive to the war's nature and the author's intent). Asa Baber sets his *The Land of a Million Elephants* (New York: Morrow, 1970) in a place of make-believe not unlike Vietnam in its geography, and quite like Vietnam in our international fantasies—fantasies which show their Western roots in Malraux's *The Royal Way* and Graham Greene's *The Quiet American* (1955) and which are as available for quotation as any text the Vietnam experience might offer. Because of this catalog and its overwhelming constraint and direction, Baber's strategists suggest that the war provides absolutely no chance for original imaginative response, which is a reaction similar to Pelfrey's but one which in Foucaultian terms speaks for an entirely different understanding of causality: that America has been so deadened by nonstop unrest, dissent, and assassination that "if you had a National Blood Pressure Monitor at the moment you heard the news you would have found virtually no response. No orgasm" (p. 95).

Baber's startling description of this lack of imaginative possibility may be closest to the truth of what the war really meant for some parts of American culture. But within the limits of actual events, it remained the role of novelists to find a structure. Dr. Ronald J. Glasser's *365 Days* (New York: Braziller, 1971) admitted the problem in virtually the same language as Ronald Sukenick's *In Form* and *The Death of the Novel and Other Stories*: "There is no novel in Nam, there is not enough for a plot, nor is there really any character development. If you survive 365 days without getting killed or wounded you simply go home and take up again where you left off" (p. xii). Yet within this artificially imposed tour of duty Glasser sketches many aspects of the war: the suicidal role of helicopter pilots, the medics' psychotic altruism, and the case of a veteran commander who against the military silliness of Vietnam applies World War II tactics with great success until he is fragged by his most decidedly Vietnam-era troops. Airmen's routines—office-hour schedules for bombing Vietnam from comfortable bases in Thailand while intimately involved in affairs back home—are used by George Davis as the structure for *Coming Home* (New York: Random House, 1971), another Sukenick-like device for turning the problem with form into a solution. No wonder Davis's black officer decides that "this war is like Harvard. Nothing in it seems real. Everything is abstract. Everything is an argument or a question" (p. 77).

In terms of structuring such an elusive subject, the most successful novel to portray the military situation in Vietnam is Josiah Bunting's *The Lionheads* (New York: Braziller, 1972). A former command officer in Vietnam teaching history at West Point when his book was published, Bunting comprehends and expresses the Vietnam situation simply by discussing it within the traditional form of army chain-of-command, an approach as valid as any phenomenological examination of the surface, as free as one can ever hope to be from the anthropomorphical projections of one's own attitudes, prejudices, and factually groundless presuppositions. Bunting's novel starts at the top, where a major general knows something very important:

> that commanding a Division in the combat theatre can be the capstone of an excellent career of service, leading to one further assignment . . . or, if he truly distinguishes himself as Division Commander, the assignment will lead to another promotion—the big step to three stars (only 15 percent of two-star generals are promoted to the three star rank). . . . He wants to be Chief of Staff—of the Army. (p. 15)

So much for looking upward. With the visit of a branch secretary imminent, the general mounts a campaign, the implications of which are carried down-staff with his orders. At division he charges one of his colonels in the manner of a sales director: "Your body-count is a standing joke. Tell you what, Robertson, you have one week to produce" (p. 66). Among the three brigades there is a scramble for the division's helicopter assets; inevitably, one unit is shorted and sustains an appalling number of deaths. But spread among all the forces, overall casualties are sufficiently acceptable for the general to claim a significant victory. As the battle has progressed from planning through preparation to execution, Bunting has followed the action down through brigade, batallion, and company to platoon and squad, until he reaches what the army calls the "real sharp individual"—the soldier in the field, in this case PFC Compella, the single person in the book devoid of all but purely human ambition. In the first chapter, at division, he has been temporarily assigned as an aide, displaying maps for the coming battle. "PFC Compella notes that the officers take no notice of him, but follow only the movements of the tip of the pointer as it plots the new locations on the briefing map" (p. 6), which is Bunting's advice to the reader on how the method of his book will proceed, touching upon but steadfastly refusing to allow for any "human" element in this system, no matter how compelling those human elements may prove to be. One compassionate colonel's worry about the war, its strategy, and its tactics will count for nothing, no matter how much the author's or the reader's heart bleeds for him, because the system has become its own reality (and henceforth the only solid ground on which the novelist can build his or her world). As for Private Compella, his presence is as unreal as is any presence deconstructed by Derrida—he occupies the briefing room only as a trace of those deaths orchestrated by the commanders attending to his map-pointer. At the novel's conclusion, when he himself is the fine point of the war's action, the officers again take no note of him, for he is killed on a day for rejoicing, when casualties are moderate instead of heavy or catastrophic or otherwise unacceptable, making his personal erasure thoroughly acceptable; his removal leaves only a deconstructive trace which marks his experience in Vietnam as absolute but inconceivable in conventional terms.

In this manner the Vietnam experience remains humanly unmeasurable to the military. For army veterans writing and publishing fiction during the war's active years, the experience made little sense. Confused sergeants, whose twenty years of service span the end of World War II, Korea, and the beginnings of Vietnam, are familiar characters in novels emerging from the war—and in very few cases do they find a solution to or even an understanding of what is going on. The larger dimensions remain the province of professional writers—who may or may not be vets, but whose commitment to fiction preceded Vietnam and whose careers have eclipsed its subject in the aftermath. Two novelists of this generation wrote their first books about the war: James Park Sloan with *War Games* (Boston: Houghton Mifflin, 1971) and William Crawford Woods with *The Killing Zone* (New York:

Harper's Magazine Press/Harper & Row, 1970). Sloan, from a prominent military family in South Carolina, took time off from his honors program degree at Harvard to enlist in the army, train as a paratrooper, and request duty in Vietnam so that he could test his theories about structuring a war novel in postmodern times. Woods, a Signal Corps veteran of the Far East Network with a graduate degree from Johns Hopkins, saw Vietnam as a similar challenge for structuring the void in terms of a subject matter including but reaching far beyond the war; his concerns would include artificial languages and technological essences which contribute to the style of "experimental realism" that characterizes fiction others have come to write nearly a quarter century after the first American advisers started carrying arms in Vietnam.

War Games begins with its narrator's attempt to write the novel at hand, by 1971 a familiar device employed by Ronald Sukenick, Steve Katz, and other radical innovators back home in order to suspend the suspension of disbelief and redirect attention to the unstructurability of content which refused to be pliably mimetic. In Sloan's case, however, his protagonist is not only writing a novel, but he has joined the army to learn how to write it. The real Vietnam-era infantry will provide field experience for the test of two theories:

> *Theory One*
>
> The timid hero goes to Vietnam like a sissy dipping his toe in the pool. Suddenly he realizes that he can be a cold-water swimmer. This happens because Vietnam provides him with a character-molding experience. It is both purposeful and earthshaking. There is a flash of insight. He realizes that he is now fully mature. He has become a soldier and a man.
>
> This is only a hypothesis. Then there is Theory Two.
>
> *Theory Two*
>
> A tough-minded young man, who unsuspectingly has above-average sensitivity, goes to Vietnam. For the first time in his life he encounters genuine brutality and tragedy—perhaps his first tragic love affair. This experience shocks him into his own humanity. There is a flash of insight. He comes home in total revulsion at war and probably writes a book. (p. 4)

These two projections are, of course, deliberately filled with the claptrap of an outworn tradition already successfully demolished by Sukenick and Katz, and philosophically discredited by Barthes and Derrida. But rehearsing those demolitions—from the vagaries of character, through the coincidence of insightful epiphanies, to the structural implications of youth and maturity, innocence and experience, the second version of which results in yet another book—gives Sloan only the first two pages of his own novel. To write on, something else must be done; and so, in a Beckettian tradition of "I can't go on. I'll go on," Sloan allows his narrator to proceed with whatever structures might be at hand, constructing—like a French *bricoleur*—a makeshift pattern which, one way or another, will get the job done.

The first such structure is his service dental chart, an extremely important document that will accompany him through life as the army remains responsible for all adjacent teeth. Quite logically, the narrator has devised a plan to spend his year in Vietnam systematically requesting work on every third tooth in his mouth. As does Josiah Bunting in *The Lionheads,* Sloan reminds us that systems displace us from one reality by offering the presumed stability of another—and that in each case what has been "real" is only the system itself. Is a dental chart any less real than the command structure of the army, reaching down from division while looking up toward the Joint Chiefs and the Department of Defense (and, above that, State, Congress, the Presidency, and the democracy they supposedly serve)? That Sloan even asks indicates that it is less real than it is provisional; that he does ask proves the radical nature of his narrative, which structures the void by employing the most cosmically pedestrian yet personally consequential device for order.

This dental chart turns out to be the most rational plan in the novel. Like other writers before him, Sloan finds that there are many unreal things in this new war: troop-carrying luxury airliners that race the sun across the Pacific, serving breakfast by the clock every hour; APO mail that sends the same letter around the world twenty-seven times; a peacetime army staffed by uniformed civil servants who must suddenly and quite literally fight for their careers; and dozens of other incongruities that suggest how Vietnam and the war are a world apart from anything America has previously known. Officially, the army contrives its own unreality to match this state of affairs. As David Halberstam's Captain Beaupré learned four years earlier, it is a non-linear war, with no objective to seize, no identifiable goal to achieve, and no overall end-date in sight:

Each departure is festive in its own way. Since there has been no mass homecoming, it seems that each individual's leaving must represent a victory in miniature. Since the rotations after one-year tours are staggered, victory is a continuous process. It is thus more sustained than the sword tendering, paper signing, and ticker-tape marching of previous wars. On the other hand, it is followed by an equally continuous reappraisal. Newcomers are always groaning that "that bastard left me in a bind." (p. 40)

The service treats it as a game, and Sloan's clerk-protagonist soon masters it as a modal exercise, keeping the body counts at a steady three-to-one ratio in our favor—"Which is good, but not good enough. Any worse and there would be alarm. Any better and the statistics would be checked" (p. 87). Needless to say, he never bothers with the facts, simply maintaining a list of monthly battles as random towns come up from the roster he's compiled. Everyone else is happy, no one suffers physical damage from these actions, and the war in Vietnam proceeds pretty much as it has, with the real killing and destruction safely off his chart and out of his world.

For the first half of *War Games,* there is no war in Vietnam as contemporary television accounts reported it. And so Sloan's narrator is frustrated in his attempt to test his novel-writing theories with some firsthand combat experience, learning instead that wars "are reserved to those who do not want to go" (p. 98). For most of the novel's initial fifteen of thirty short chapters, he has been in the position of a frustrated Hamlet who "must devise the play, then act in it" (p. 9). As he makes progress through his war, he advances from pretexts (his study of *A Farewell to Arms, All Quiet on the Western Front,* and *The Red Badge of Courage*) to subtexts (the actual literary structures of the war, from phony machine-written letters of commendation to his own battle charts). Soon it seems like he is writing a novel, even as the frustrations at not getting into combat prompt him to wonder if he may be inventing too many things, his actual life now merging with his artistic imagination. Soon his imagination does triumph over reality, but in a decidedly amoral way: allowed to walk patrol with a group of South Vietnamese Rangers, he becomes sickened by his allies' torture of innocent villagers and the sexual mutilation of their animals. Setting his rifle on automatic fire and following up with a grenade, he destroys them all, ARVN soldiers, villagers, and animals alike—a triumph of indiscriminate vengeance worthy of Sloan's mentor at the time, novelist Jerzy Kosinski. For this act the narrator expects to be court-martialed and executed, just as Sloan risks the disapprobation heaped on Kosinski for writing *The Painted Bird* (1965) and *Steps* (1968), but the narrator of *War Games* feels he has at least performed a significant act in this otherwise nonsignifying war.

The writer and his "small war" (working title for both his and Sloan's novel) are saved by his new boss, Colonel Rachow, who has authored the army manual *Creative Leadership and Collective Tunnel Vision,* and who in other times "would have been magnificent . . . as a papal lawyer in the twelfth century. Or perhaps as the head of a noble family encroaching on its vassals." Rachow sympathizes with the protagonist's behavior because he can articulate many of the young soldier's feelings about the unreal war against Vietnam, as he extrapolates from a classic Bismarckian, Napoleonic, Stonewall Jackson-like plan for invading Canada to a textual strategy right out of low-grade science fiction:

> War, said Rachow, has ceased to be tied down by facts. It has become metaphysical; one might say a platonic form. He asked me to picture an amphibious landing across Lake Michigan. Then imagine, he said, such things as landings by Martians; invaders from liquid planets formed of molten lava, surprised and threatened by our explorations. This is the future of military planning. War is no longer waged merely to achieve ends; it is waged as a proof of its own possibility. (p. 144)

Such imaginative possibilities, and their consequences, have led the protagonist to the climax of his own physical action. Now the colonel provides his clerk with a sense of creative authority for conducting the war—until Rachow destroys himself on a symbolic rescue mission, the goal of which is as textually abstract as any of his manuals, yet is accomplished in a personally heroic manner worthy of the finest, most traditional soldiering.

Rachow's mission has been to recover his crew-chief's body from the primeval Southeast Asian swamp André Malraux made so fatally attractive in *The Royal Way*—another text, to be sure, but in this case a text more appropriate for Rachow than the outdated war stories Sloan's protagonist has read before his tour. That mission fails, but its failure provides the climax for the narrator's own story, allowing *War Games* to be written in the form the reader now reads—in literary terms, the ultimate sacrifice of authorial self to the intertext.

William Crawford Woods' *The Killing Zone* complements this form of resolution by employing even more artifice in order to come to terms with this most artificial of wars. A confused sergeant stands at the center of this novel's action, which takes place not in Vietnam but rather in a New Jersey training camp where the tactics of the war are rehearsed. Sergeant Melton, an old-fashioned combat hero from World War II, has rejected the field commission and careerist promotions that would have led him, over the years, into Josiah Bunting's managerial officer caste of the 1960s. Instead, he finds himself first sergeant of a company with no executive officer, its C.O. having been felled by a heart attack on the golf course a few days before. And so he is in a position of command when a new first lieutenant arrives to test a demonstration plan of computerized warfare—a plan inspired by the Vietnam War for which the inductees are training. The war and its methods are like no other, and the lieutenant helping to plan them is equally new:

> Twenty-four years old. BS and MS in electrical engineering from the University of California. Master's thesis on some military application of information retrieval. ROTC commission deferred until after graduate school. Part-time programmer for Armed Resources Corporation—one of those ambiguous concerns that hide in the rolling countryside of Maryland and Virginia within fifteen minutes by chopper of the Pentagon; semisecret compounds where men in short-sleeved white voile shirts translate Defense Department contracts into Fortran and the other tongues of Babel, and learn from the shimmering surfaces of their machines how to move the elements of war in an ordered march across the chessboard of the earth. (p. 5)

Unlike James Park Sloan's protagonist who generates his own narrative possibilities out of the intertext of literary war, Woods's Lieutenant Track privileges speech over writing—what the deconstructionists would declare is a classic error, sure to invite the style of destruction inevitable when artificial authority is given the mystique of naturalistic presence. In *The Killing Zone* his specialty is to see how closely and how well a computer can perform with a small line unit in a rapidly changing combat situation. The unit chosen for this experiment is led by a Vietnam veteran, Sergeant Cox, who is of Track's age but who is in spirit more akin to Melton's army. Despite the strange nature of the war and the even more incongruous circumstances in which one trains for it—"the training area . . . was a parking lot; they were learning to kill like cavemen in a place where the pizza truck would stop that night" (p. 25)—Sergeant Cox resists computerized warfare and the artificial language of authority in favor of the highly personal virtues of pure soldiery, an ideal Josiah Bunting's novel admired but ultimately had to discount as unachievable in the Vietnam-era army.

Track's computer plans the action, issues plastic-headed wargame ammunition, and follows the training exercise with all the deliberation of a company commander, receiving information from the field and determining the best strategies to continue. Lieutenant Track, of course, holds such responsibility only by virtue of the flimsiest authority, the artifice of his cybernetic language; the true commander is Sergeant Melton, who can remain only as a disapproving but temporarily ineffective presence, a trace of World War II's experience on the featureless face of Vietnam. Not surprisingly, an error is made; the operator has failed to routinely clear the computer's memory storage, and as a result two boxes of live ammunition are being used. There is no way the computer itself can discover or correct its action, and Lieutenant Track's authority deteriorates into a nightmare of slaughter. How can it be stopped? That remains the prerogative of the common foot soldier, in this case Sergeant Cox, who has but one way to save his men from annihilation:

> He had been hit four times by the gunner who was still firing when he reached him. Mr. Track's computer had provided an unbeatable realism which had gone into his belly, and one bit of the realism had ruined his left arm, taken it out altogether. So it was with his rifle in one hand that he came over the barrel, calm, indifferently, almost sweetly, and with practiced smoothness and precision slid the bayonet into the boy's chest, up to the hilt, not seeing the frightened and finally knowing face glance down at the explosion of blood as cloth and skin and muscle and then bone gave way to the rushing pouring steel. Cox's finger jerked on the

trigger and a short stream of plastic bullets squirted into the open wound, splashed hot into the welling lake of blood. The sergeant and the private fell together behind the finally silent gun. (p. 164)

Unlike William Pelfrey, William Crawford Woods has found a Vietnam War era context for valid writing in the older heroic style of World War II. And unlike James Park Sloan, Woods is able to devise a situation in which the heroism can make arguable moral claims, for Cox's mortal action in the killing zone has saved what remains of his platoon even as it deals with "the real thing—the final mission of the infantry" (p. 166)—which is to kill before being killed oneself. Lieutenant Track fumbles for an excuse. Sergeant Melton, in the posture of judgment, weeps. Sergeant Cox, the single Vietnam veteran foregrounded in the novel, does what you do in the infantry.

Because he has attacked the technology itself and discredited the false authority of Lieutenant Track's artificial language, Sergeant Cox can affirm both himself and the real matter of death, each of which the military technicians of the Vietnam War try to efface. *The Killing Zone* stands as the best novel to define, amid the surreal confusion of a war planned by computers and practiced in parking lots, what field remains for honor. The villains are those who disavow such honor, whether they be technocrat lieutenants who fight weekday wars with Friday night and the rest of the weekend in New York, or a military establishment that has lost sight of the purpose of soldiering. Again, it is the sergeants, young and old, who suffer even when they survive. But in Woods's novel their acts have meaning and their minds comprehend the meaning of what's going on. The lieutenant can drive away in his red Corvette, radio blaring; the first sergeant remains, to write letters of bereavement but also to understand the language that articulates these events and the intertext out of which they have emerged: "Melton paused, because the melody from Track's radio was surfacing in his mind, and he wanted to name it. It mingled with the others, then came clearer. Rock-and-roll, or what they now called just rock, the new music—he hated most of it—but he had heard before, and liked, this quiet tune: there it was: "Ruby Tuesday," by the Rolling Stones. A really beautiful song" (p. 179).

"Vietnam. Vietnam. Vietnam. There it is." James S. Kunen's closing words in his *Standard Operating Procedure: Notes of a Draft-Age*

American (New York: Avon, 1971) reiterate the difficulty of writing about this war. Existence not only precedes essence—there is no essence at all, just an incomprehensible void whose content exists only in the act of trying to structure it. Just as some military strategists argue that the lessons taught to us again and again, from Tet to Saigon, were learned by the French much earlier along the road to Dien Bien Phu, so can the literary critic suggest that writing a novel about the Vietnam War would be no easier than writing a valid novel about anything else during this transition to the full popular effect of the postmodern age. One should not forget that the first Western novelist to aesthetically structure events in this part of the world was André Malraux, who as early as 1930 saw that the Indochina experience could be a metaphor for man's alienation from an absurd society within a meaningless universe. One-third of a century later, as American writers began to struggle with the same subject matter, it would certainly be a mistake to merely replicate Malraux's themes and forms, which are the standard modernist response. By the mid-1960s Malraux's anguished alienation had become a full-blown nightmare, with literature struggling to catch up; as Norman Mailer said at the time, "If World War II was like *Catch-22*, this war will be like *Naked Lunch*" (*Cannibals and Christians* [New York: Dial Press, 1966], p. 85). The processes of art inevitably tell us more about ourselves than about the matter at hand, but for Malraux the Indochina experience was especially revealing. In the jungles of what we now call Thailand, Cambodia, and the Socialist Republic of Vietnam, he explored the roots of what two subsequent generations of novelist must face as the modernist pretext: "that fabulous aura of scandal, fantasy, and fiction which always hovers about the white man who has played a part in the affairs of independent Asiatic states" (p. 7). The jungle itself is a strange and exotic contrast to the civilizations of the West, a place where Malraux's protagonist finds that he was "growing aware of the essential oneness of the forest and had given up trying to distinguish living beings from their setting, life that moves from life that oozes" (p. 101).

Like most modernist heroes, Malraux's adventurer disappears into the heart of darkness, engulfed by what he feels are its irresistible temptations and gratifications of military power and female flesh. Twenty-five years later another Westerner, Graham Greene, places a quiet young American in a mid-1950s version of these same circumstances, where well-meaning innocence falls victim to outdated but still operative textuality. Consider this influence which Greene's story-teller finds enfolded in the narrative of *The Quiet American* (New York: Viking Press, 1956):

> I said good night to him and went into the cinema next door— Errol Flynn, or it may have been Tyrone Power (I don't know how to distinguish them in tights), swung on ropes and leaped from balconies and rode bareback into Technicolor dawns. He rescued a girl and killed his enemy and led a charmed life. It was what they call a film for boys, but the sight of Oedipus emerging with his bleeding eyeballs from the palace at Thebes would surely give a better training for life today. No life is charmed. (p. 240)

Greene's British journalist admits he cannot decipher the particulars of these texts, especially as they encode the protagonist's true identity. But he does know that Pyle, the quiet American, is a captive of them, innocently naive as he is. "I wish sometimes you had a few bad motives," he tells him; "you might understand a little more about human beings. And that applies to our country too, Pyle" (p. 173).

Yet Greene's prescriptive structure, that of the veteran journalist instructing the novice Agency for International Development man from a skeptical, loss-of-empire position, has proven no more ade-quate to the essentially postmodern experience of Vietnam than has Malraux's modernist caution. Appropriate fictive responses to Amer-ica's involvement in Vietnam will only be successful when they account for postmodern and not merely modernist techniques for dealing with a fundamentally unstructurable reality. What happens when outdated modes are pressed back into service are novels like Pelfrey's *The Big V* and, back home, Bobbie Ann Mason's *In Country* (1985) and Jayne Anne Phillips' *Machine Dreams* (1984). Mason and Phillips are espe-cially invidious in their use of an unexamined social realism, an ap-proach which manages to contextualize American actions in Vietnam without properly describing them, much less understanding the prob-lems involved with structuring a void. Both novelists rely upon the hackneyed formula of "family sagas," here adapted not to the unstruc-turability of Vietnam but rather trimmed to the contemporary MFA workshop style which has also gone by the names of Minimalism, Dirty Realism, New Realism, Pop Realism, Post-Alcoholic Blue-Collar Hyperrealism, Designer Realism, and TV Fiction, all of which regress to structural formats predating the postmodern transformation. Each novel or story in this mode seems like another van running over Roland Barthes one more time, as the patiently learned principles of literary postmodernism are bumped aside in favor of an easily teachable, writable, salable, and readable commodity that keeps all work stations in the production chain operating at blissful peak efficiency. In their popularized humanistic rereading of postmodernism, Mason and Phillips imply that Vietnam was really like any other war in the literary canon from *The Iliad* through *War and Peace* to anything James Jones may have read from at the University of Iowa Writers Workshop. Mythology, however incorrect and however subject to its controls, does work very well when it comes to flights of classroom inspiration, virtuoso displays of literary craftsmanship, attractively marketed books, and comfortably reassuring "good reads." What is lost is the special nature of the subject and its very special demands for structure, given that its substance is that of a void resistant to all previous stereotypes.

As the immediacy of Vietnam fades, the war becomes trivialized. For some it is all movies now, and the movies themselves have stepped back from an honest sense of confusion with this new reality to a reliance upon the older, standardized myths of brutality and honor which have satisfied human imaginations for millennia when it comes to questioning the meaning of war. The years of America's immediate involvement in Vietnam were also the years of our country's immediate involvement with fictive experimentation; but in the years since the fall of Saigon the practice of a new fiction has for the time surrendered to a canonical form of expression which guarantees that all the right parts in all the right places will generate appropriate critical response and readerly pleasure. The next decade's challenge will be that of a new style of realism, which by its very definition should prevent such abuse. *Experimental realism* is what it will be called, since in the hands of domestic writers such as Stephen Dixon, Grace Paley, and Walter Abish it has already shown how the conventions of literary realism can be used in an opaque, self-apparent way, so that the recession of conventionally unstructurable subject materials like Vietnam need not reopen the doors to the transparency of form and presupposed structure realistic authors used before.

For fiction of the Vietnam War, experimental realism may take yet another decade, considering how Vonnegut and Heller needed two decades and more after World War II to find a way to write their novels about those events. History presents immediate challenges, then recedes into myth. Myths for a time constrain and then are deconstructed to reveal that their naturalized systems have only posed as truths. This deconstruction is the function of artists, and here is where the truth of our culture's experience with the Vietnam War will some day be found.

7

Beyond

Time's Constraint:

Spatial Form

How does fiction speak about a subject when subject matter is said to exist not in itself but only as an absence postulated by a system of differences and exclusions? When facing earlier challenges to its nature, fiction has responded by emphasizing its spatial rather than temporal nature. For a medium whose chief feature is that of narrative, such a focus threatens to undo its substance. Yet in today's deconstructionist climate of difference and absence the spatial concept of various states existing in simultaneity rather than sequence is an attractive one, for it allows one to envision all those differences not as separate takes but as a coherent and instantaneous whole.

Fiction's suitability for such a vision was established by Joseph Frank in his seminal essays on spatial form, later collected in *The Widening Gyre: Crisis and Mastery in Modern Literature* (New Brunswick, N.J.: Rutgers University Press, 1963). Frank himself began with a critical awareness of the physical challenge, that juxtaposing word groups for simultaneous perception and suspending the process of individual reference until the entire pattern of such references could be apprehended as a unity are much easier to manage in a poem, where the entire text confronts the reader's vision, than in a narrative of several hundred pages. Frank also reminds us that these difficulties exist primarily in theory, because there are many famously successful works of fiction that derive their proper understanding by virtue of just such perception. The market-fair scene in *Madame Bovary* is his favorite example, for without any damage to the reader's imagination a great number of diverse temporal actions are suspended in one magnificently spatial scene. And reading Frank's analysis of that scene today, in a world reeducated by Derrida and other philosophers and theorists, one hears a critical language that sounds eminently postmodern, as for the duration of the market-fair scene "the time-flow of the narrative is halted; attention is fixed on the interplay of relationships within the immobilized time area. These relationships are juxtaposed independently of the progress of the narrative, and the full significance of the scene is given only in the reflexive relationships among the units of meaning" (p. 15).

The reason for the scene's success points to a factor common in postmodern fiction: that the action captured is present not in narrative movement or sequence, but rather as an artifact in itself, something that the writing and then the reading have *made* from all the diverse items mentioned. The resultant fiction thus seeks not to imitate an action that has taken place in the world, but instead to create the very elements of action, which then develop a story within the reader's imagination—not on the page of recorded history, with its dependence upon time and sequence, cause and effect, and of course essential subjecthood.

Within his more specifically limited purposes Frank described a scene that stands independent of time, with no antecedents or consequences in the narrative. The ideal spatial fiction, then, would be an entire novel that conformed to this pattern. Such a work would have to be absolved of representing some action in the world; even more so, it should not have to represent some other, secondhand reality at all, but rather be its own reality, where the reader's pleasure is not to recognize the artful depiction of some familiar world but to appreciate the element of this new work's composition, which just as in viewing a painting would be a spatially organized affair. Narrative succession itself is not the culprit in debasing spatial form in fiction. The true problem is the illusion of such predisposed succession, which forces the reader to absorb a work in only one way, with attention to the sequence of developments distracting from the compositional act. It is not time itself that must collapse, but *illusionary* time, just as it is not space itself that collapses in certain Cubist and Futurist paintings but just illusionary space (as used in perspective painting). In each case by getting rid of the illusion the work establishes a validity in its own right rather than as a reflection of something else.

When subject matter becomes not a thing representable in itself but only an activity suggested by absence and a system of differences, the fiction writer's path toward spatial form becomes a clear one. The key distinction is one's attitude toward verisimilitude. In traditional fiction that would seek to represent a subject, verisimilitude is based on time rather than space, because the novelist's aim in such work is to demonstrate the "realistic" qualities of life in action, in life as it happens in represented form—which means in sequence, in causality, and therefore in time. As Ronald Sukenick suggests in *In Form: Digressions on the Act of Fiction* (Carbondale: Southern Illinois University Press, 1985), by asking the reader to suspend disbelief in favor of illusion "one can make an image of the real thing which, though not real, is such a persuasive likeness that it can represent our control over reality" (pp. 3–4). Yet when reality itself is just an arbitrary convention, constructed as idiosyncratically as any one culture might determine, the whole issue of control is shifted from an emphasis on the convincingness of the subject as represented to the authority of the artist as creator. The work therefore no longer unfolds in time as an illusion in which the reader participates but structures itself in space as a composition the writer has made—a work that is not complete until all parts are in place.

The modern period made much progress beyond realism and naturalism, but looking back at Joseph Frank's critique of the period we see why it was unable to produce a spatial-form fiction unfettered by the claims of time. "If there is one theme that dominates the history of modern culture since the last quarter of the nineteenth century," Frank suggests, "it is precisely that of insecurity, instability, the feeling of loss of control over the meaning and purpose of life amidst the continuing triumphs of science and technics" (p. 55). Cultures at ease with their anthropological description of the world produce naturalism; those at odds with their perception of the environment tend toward abstraction and nonrealistic forms. But the modern period, as Frank shows, was in its very rebellion against external authority quite conscious of its own alienation from it. The modernists' center of meaning, informing the value of their aesthetics, remains in the empirical, documentary world, for even as such writers describe their alienation from it, the basis of their art remains the sequential time as exhibited by that world in process. Of Pound's *Cantos* and other "peculiarly modern" works that Frank sees as having spatial form, he remarks that "all maintain a continual juxtaposition between aspects of the past and the present so that both [past and present] are fused in one comprehensive view"

(p. 59). Only by moving so elusively within the bounds of historical time does spatial-form fiction have the chance to slip away from temporality's grasp.

In structuring the void of subject matter, postmodern fiction disavows historical time entirely, depending upon no reference to the temporal world other than as one factor among many in composition. The modernists transformed experience into myth—for which, as Frank says, historical time does not exist. Yet such myth serves as a subject in itself, the deepest reality underlying the historically real, an absolute of absolutes, which limits the spatial freedom of fiction even more strictly than temporal need. Myth should be treated as an arbitrarily constructed order superimposed upon existence to give that existence meaning. But as meaning is achieved, the conventional nature of myth is replaced by an absolute dependency upon it to enforce that meaning. As Roland Barthes was fond of showing and as deconstruction itself is dedicated to exposing, conventional meaning becomes naturalized. Untenable assumptions stand behind everything held true and dear, which as an unacknowledged situation guarantees alienation and ultimate discord. Yet by such dependence upon myth art becomes far less of an artificial act of composition and more of an imitation of a preexisting realm. Whether real or ideal, the result is the same—for in terms of representation, which both the real and the ideal demand, *eternal* is no less tyrannical than *temporal*. The point of art becomes corrupted, forcing it to be not something in itself but something else, making the last chance to structure a void impossible. An idea, which is just as dependent upon temporal representation as is any action, becomes the point of art—and, as a subject, becomes philosophically impossible to achieve. Instead of as Barthes's infinitely layered onion, whose sense exists in its textured layerings, one views the artwork as an encapsulation of truth, a nut one must crack in search of its kernel of truth. The components of fiction thus collapse themselves in the service of this kernel, as human qualities are refined into character, character into the pursuit of action, action structured in a plot, and the plot itself reduced to the explication of the idea the writer has supposedly encapsulized. As components, these features fall away as one moves through them, almost transparently, toward the key idea. What remains is the movement, and that movement is a slave to represented time.

When fiction is about something else, as happens when there is an explicit idea or meaning behind the work, what results is the dramatization of that idea through story. And once that happens, the possibilities for space are limited. Action becomes more important than setting, while space becomes the servant of time rather than a locus that might well structure its being. As postmodern fiction struggles with this dilemma, writers find that the struggle itself allows them to both face these problems (without always resolving them) yet complete a work that almost has it both ways. Robert Coover's *The Universal Baseball Association, Inc., J. Henry Waugh, Prop.* (New York: Random House, 1968) uses the device of a card-table baseball game to show how one element (the temporally real world of the game player) can be counterpointed effectively with the other (the spatially artificial world of the tabletop game itself). Coover solves the modernist problem of encapsulation by locating the *idea* in the first realm, where it more properly belongs (as the narrative is self-consciously manipulated), leaving the story of the game itself as pure and self-evident artifice, representing nothing other than itself. Other fictions use deliberately temporal elements, such as a journey, to emphasize not the passage of time but the structural properties of space. Gilbert Sorrentino's *The Sky Changes* (New York: Hill & Wang, 1966) adopts the form of a cross-country trip as the vehicle for the protagonist to piece together why his marriage has disintegrated, but the successions of times and places are meaningless in terms of history and even geography and are in fact deliberately thrown out of order to emphasize both the stasis of his mind and their compositional purpose as the author probes that stasis. Sorrentino's novel set in a Brooklyn neighborhood, *Steelwork* (New York: Pantheon, 1970), again mixes many different times and places so that the reader may construct an imaginative (rather than strictly historical) picture of the area, a picture that is independent of the vicissitudes of time and the ravages of temporal progress over space: a dozen different street corners and a dozen different years come together to form a single image, which in itself, apart from all the changes, constitutes a realization of this space (in which space rather than time is allowed to dominate).

Successful spatial-form fiction must create its own meaning out of the artifice of fiction, having compositional elements do the work otherwise assigned to externally imposed meaning (itself derived from the work's putative "idea"). "As artifice," Sukenick writes in *In Form,* "the work of art is a conscious tautology in which there is always an implicit (and sometimes explicit) reference to its own nature as artifact—self-reflexive, not self-reflective. It is not an imitation but a new thing in its own right, an invention" (p. 29). The artist must believe absolutely in the reality of his or her work; otherwise it dissolves into irony or parody, the literature of exhaustion written by John Barth and Thomas Pynchon, who are caught in the dilemma of realizing how futile it is to represent something in their literature but lacking confidence in their own works as real. The poetic truth of fiction is, according to Sukenick, "a statement of a particular rapport with reality sufficiently persuasive that we may for a time share it"—here, for sure, is a refuge against pure abstraction or utter meaninglessness. But note his qualification: "This kind of 'truth' does not depend upon an accurate description of 'reality' but rather itself generates what we call reality, reordering our perceptions and sustaining a vital connection to the world" (p. 31). It is noteworthy that Jean-Paul Sartre shared this same notion of fiction's generative role, since Joseph Frank speculated that existentialist philosophy may have contributed to the increased interest in spatial form. In *Imagination* (Ann Arbor: University of Michigan Press, 1962, trans. Forrest Williams) Sartre distinguishes the fictive act from simple perception, arguing that "All fictions would be active syntheses, products of our free spontaneity, and all perceptions, on the contrary, would be purely passive syntheses. The difference between fictional images and perceptions would therefore spring from the fundamental structures of intentional syntheses" (p. 142).

Intentionality becomes all; the artwork is no longer envisioned, as by Michelangelo, imprisoned within the blocks of unshaped marble awaiting his release, but as a structure put together by the artist's mind, much as John Cage organizes the elements given him by his aleatory resources. Therefore what was spatially impossible for modernist and earlier literatures becomes a possibility for postmodern work. The difference is as obvious as the contrast between James Joyce's images of motion and Alain Robbe-Grillet's use of spatial relationships, an emphasis (in deconstructive terms) of its existence within a system of differences and therefore, constructed as these differences are, a work that proclaims its own fictionality (as opposed to Joyce's which almost always implies the substructure of myth). Because Robbe-Grillet's fictive world avoids humanizing metaphors, it brooks none of the restrictions of time that influence conventional fiction and avoids the pathetic fallacy that Jerzy Peterkiewicz describes in *The Other Side of Silence: The Poet at the Limits of Language*

(London: Oxford University Press, 1970), the fallacy that invokes "the 'tragification of the universe,' either in the form of despair at the discovery that the external world does not after all contain the human meaningfulness with which it has been invested, or in the form of a cynical acceptance that this world is meaningless and therefore absurd" (p. 66).

From Roland Barthes we learn how the efforts of later *nouveau* romancers, notably Michel Butor, extend the range of fiction toward pure spatiality. Butor's *Mobile* makes no attempt to dramatize theme, a temporal affair, but rather chooses a purely combinatory variety for its narrative. "The units of discourse," Barthes observes in *Critical Essays* (Evanston: Northwestern University Press, 1972, trans. Richard Howard), are "essentially defined by their function (in the mathematical sense of the term), not by their rhetorical nature: a metaphor exists in itself; a structural unit exists only by distribution, i.e., by relation to other units." The resulting work of fiction, then, is distinguished by a movement "of perpetual transmission, not of internal 'growth'" (p. 181). Plot, that servant of time, recedes under the weight of spatially described objects, which are energized not by their enforced movement on the page but by their actualization in the reader's mind as it breaks the code of composition. Barthes makes his point in *Writing Degree Zero* (Boston: Beacon Press, 1970, trans. Annette Lavers and Colon Smith): "It is now writing which absorbs the whole identity of a literary work" (p. 85).

Barthes's energization can be seen in a wide variety of American short stories and novels, from Stephen Dixon's narratives that develop a universe of activities not by external reference but by complications from and recombinations of their original elements to the more graphically material devices used by Ronald Sukenick (including paragraphs successively one-line shorter with intervening spaces one line longer, all of which are impelled forward by run-on sentences) and Walter Abish (who has composed narratives by arranging first sentences from famous texts and generated his own by means of expanding and contracting the alphabet—making all the words in Chapter A begin with that letter, in Chapter B with words commencing with "a" and "b," and so forth up and down the alphabet). Sukenick describes it as the difference between an imposed order and one that develops as it goes along; such development, while allowing temporal succession, relies on spatial juxtaposition for its structure, just as a jazz musician's improvised solo asks the listener to compare and contrast the shape of his present line with what has gone before and with what looms forever in the background (the original melody, structured by the defining chords).

Thus the invalidity of fiction's subject matter has not stopped the production of fiction, but only reemphasized its productive as opposed to reflective properties. From Kurt Vonnegut's use of autobiography and Max Apple's employment of ritual as generators of narrative, through the more specifically technical developments within comedy and the constraints of gender and war, we have seen the structuring impulse move closer and closer to a hard materiality of its own, climaxing in the palpable shape of spatial form as contemporary writers achieve in almost routine practice what their predecessors projected only as an ideal.

Significantly, nowhere in this process has the substance of fiction disappeared. Rather than fly up its own narrowing gyre of metafictive practice, as some critics once feared, novels and short stories of our time have been able to remain pertinent to the world even as the very success of their techniques keeps readers employed within the constituent structuring activities that makes such fiction happen. The path this resolution has taken, given its spatial emphasis, is much like the course of painting in the century's second half, for there too the initial exuberances of abstract expressionism made some critics fear that art would no longer be relevant to the state of the world or to anything beyond the artist's own activity. As the century winds down to its end, we have seen that what began as a mandate for abstraction, with virtually no representation of a recognizable world, resolves itself in something looking much like realism and bearing that critical appellation in its title—photorealism in painting, neorealism in fiction.

The parallels work out in both critical and practical realms. What Roland Barthes says about the generative nature of narrative recalls statements made by art critics from Harold Rosenberg to Frank O'Hara during the decade of abstract expressionism's ascendancy, and just as the painterly techniques of Jackson Pollock and Willem de Kooning correspond to the fictive achievements of Ronald Sukenick, a photorealistic canvas by Richard Estes will employ the same generative principles as an otherwise realistic story by Stephen Dixon. Most importantly, the integrity of the critical system that proposes a theory for their work can be established by seeing how all four areas of activities, from the abstract expressionist canvas and the commentary that explains it to the photorealistic painting and the principles behind it, are essentially the same, making the supposedly abstract work pertinently real and the aggressive realism of the latter work representational only on the surface, for structuring its content is an approach that shares all the central beliefs of abstraction and innovation.

Of course, painting and fiction have never dealt with reality itself but rather with what a given culture sees as reality. A typical fiction by Walter Abish or Stephen Dixon and painting by Richard Estes or Ralph Goings incorporates within its vision both the new technology in our lives and the equally new modes of perception within which we see. No artist of one hundred and fifty years ago was faced with the plethora of highly polished reflective surfaces as confront Abish and Estes on every urban street corner, nor would any Victorian or Belle Epoque writer suspect that so much contemporary reality lay on the surface, or that the artistic glance might include more information than real-life perception could ever contain. New conditions and new rules for dealing with those conditions lead to different philosophies of artistic response. Yet for all the apparent difference between a Pollock canvas of splashy, tangled lines and an Estes rendition of a Walgreen's street corner, and between a Sukenick narrative deconstructing itself and a Dixon story supposedly populated by recognizable people doing customary things, there is a continuity of approach toward reality that marks these works as coming from the same culture and following the same aesthetic principles.

Comparing the painting of the early 1950s and the fiction of the later 1960s can be an exercise in the obvious, for the principle that in abstract expressionism the canvas is no longer a surface upon which to represent but an arena within which to act, yielding not a picture but an event, corresponds directly to innovative fiction's dedication not to representing an action but enacting it itself. As a line in painting is an act's manifestation, so too is a line in narrative a trace of the author's activity, particularly when it proceeds in the ongoing mode of improvisation favored by Sukenick and others. So too does fiction appreciate, rather than obliterate, the materiality of its construction: creative presence would not be something to efface but rather the substance of the work itself. Meaning thence becomes not a property of subject matter but rather of the process of composition—composition that in its spatial juxtaposition of parts enacts the system of differences that

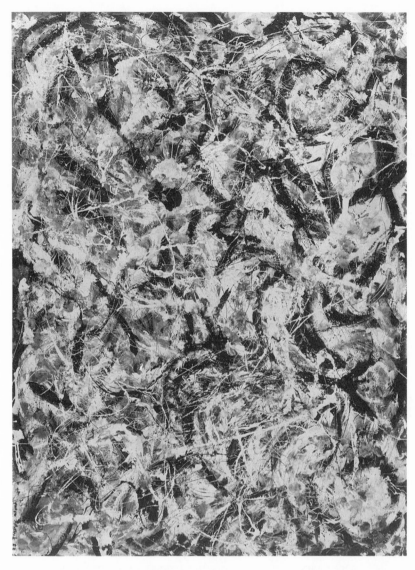

"Greyed Rainbow" by Jackson Pollock, American, *1912–1956, oil on canvas, 1953, 182.9 × 243.8 cm. Gift of the Society for Contemporary American Art, 1955.494. Photograph courtesy of The Art Institute of Chicago.*

"Drugs" by Richard Estes, American, b.1937, oil on canvas, 1970, 152.4 ×
112.7 cm. Restricted gift of Edgar Kaufmann, 1970.1100. Photograph courtesy of The Art Institute of Chicago

structures the void of subject. Action painting suggests action writing, and action writing is just what the self-reflexive novelists, notably Ronald Sukenick and his close associates, began producing in the 1960s.

Yet even as the 1990s commence and both fiction and painting reembrace supposedly figurative content, the principles of abstract expressionism and action writing still pertain, reminding one that what looks like subject matter is really something else: not an attempt to portray the void of content but rather to achieve a complete artistic work by structuring that void.

Consider the most apparent feature of abstraction, its "all over manner" which in the drip paintings of Jackson Pollock swirl from border to border with splashed colors and tangled lines. Nothing could be farther from the rubrics of realism, for the interest in such work literally fills the canvas, every inch of it, as opposed to the ordered perspective so essential to the depiction of a subject. Hans Hofmann used this same principle to display his "push and pull" of color forces on the canvas; Franz Kline used it for his arm's length gesture of black paint thrust across the white canvas, while Willem de Kooning saw it as the arena for his many-layered dance of color and impasto. A photorealistic painting embraces this same "all over" aesthetic. The urban landscapes of Richard Estes seem like expeditions in search of street corners, diners, rows of phone booths, facades, show windows, shop rows, or any other reflective surfaces conducive to the indiscriminate spread of perception over a broad, flat surface. Estes's *Drugs* defies selection as it depicts a vision of a corner pharmacy most notable for its highly polished surface, each reflective square of marble, glass, or chrome filling the canvas with a superabundance of information, a strategy that so amplifies and extends realism's role of reflecting something to the point that reflection itself becomes the feature as well as the form. An upstairs window is painted with the same precision as the central display cases—understandably so, because each pane of glass is doing its job of mirroring whatever falls within its plane of reference, a panoply of mindless signs whose signifying process yields nothing to the hierarchy of its referent. As such, it is viewed most profitably just like a Pollock.

The "all over" nature of innovative fiction from the late 1960s and early 1970s is obvious, most notably in the ongoing effect of Ronald Sukenick's work. But neorealistic works of the 1980s and 1990s follow the same principle, especially as Stephen Dixon takes the redundant problems of realism (akin to Estes's surfaces that exist only to reflect, but which reflect indiscriminately and overabundantly) and makes them the very form and feature of his story. A perfect example is his story "Said" from *Love and Will* (New York: Paris Review Editions/British American Publishing, 1989), where the familiar nuisance of having to identify the speaker of each line or dialogue becomes not a convention in the service of meaning but the narrative's principle feature as what the couple say is completely effaced:

> He said, she said.
> She left the room, he followed her.
> He said, she said.
> She locked herself in the bathroom, he slammed the door with his fists.
> He said.
> She said nothing.
> He said.
> He slammed the door with his fists, kicked the door bottom.
> She said, he said, she said.
> He batted the door with his shoulder, went into the kitchen, got a screwdriver, returned and started unscrewing the bathroom doorknob.
> She said. . . . (p. 99)

The convention which had seemed so instrumental for conveying content here provides content enough for an entire narrative to unfold. In the process Dixon has made that convention not a transparent signifier but, like Estes's reflective surfaces, an opaque sign, a true thing in itself. By dropping out the content that can be imagined to precede each pair of *saids*, Dixon foregoes illusionistic centering in favor of the same allover effect that characterizes both Pollock and Estes canvases and Sukenick fictions—all quite appropriate to the void he wishes to structure, in this case the substanceless nature of most marital fights. One thinks again of Estes's *Drugs*: few people can remember accurately what a corner Walgreen's looks like in its specifics, but they have a solid sense of its effect, just as it is so hard to remember what a lovers' spat was about. Each has an allover quality to its experience and qualifies as a void virtually unrepresentable as content or subject matter. Yet each has been structured in such a work.

"Antihierarchal" is the second principle shared by abstract expressionist art and innovative fiction and is also applicable to the apparently realistic work done in both media decades later. Its key is having no single compositional element take precedence over the other. In Ronald Sukenick's *Out* there are neither high points nor low points as his narrative crosses the continent, just as there are none in Gilbert Sorrentino's *The Sky Changes*. The effect of these novels is much like that of seeing Pollock's lines and splashes fill the canvas, where just as much action happens in the corners as in the center. In similar manner the tension in Hans Hofmann's work results from his energies playing themselves from one block of color against the other, none of which is privileged but all of which are equal in completing the dynamic effect. Even close inspection of a painting by de Kooning yields the same antihierarchal effect, for here the close viewer finds many layers of paint imposed upon each so thoroughly that no single plane dominates. What you see is what there is. For similar effect photorealism adopts the position of a camera, an approach so visual that it excludes intellectual prejudices toward organization and priority. Allowing for no specific focus or conceptual center of interest, the camera presents an overload of data, every detail just as sharp and clear as the rest, with lines from every square inch of surface sharpened to identical clarity. The techniques of painting allow these effects to be exaggerated, through extreme enlargement (while still maintaining sharpness) and superimposition (lumping the details of three or four photos into one painted view). Depicted content is thus maximalized to the extent that distinctions of subject are effaced. Such lack of hierarchy allows an infinity of planar focus, such as being able to look through a window and at it simultaneously. In Estes's *Central Savings* one looks through the window at objects inside, back from the window's reflection, and at a third plane of focus caught within the reflected surface behind one across the street. In terms of perception the view can go on forever, just as one of Stephen Dixon's stories is so self-generative that it can be ended only by a mechanical device: closing one's eyes or going to sleep, so that no more action can be generated from the materials at hand.

"Through the avoidance of a hierarchy that is related to values outside the actual work, language has a chance of becoming what Roland Barthes refers to as a field of action"—so Walter Abish describes this same principle's use for fiction, in his *Fiction International* interview from fall 1975 (p. 95). Note the distinction: not an avoidance of figurative material, but of values outside the actual work. Hence Dixon can write figurative stories in this manner if he restricts himself to advances of narrative generated by the original figures and not by introducing new concerns along the way, such as meaning-directed realism would. Antihierarchal means divesting signs of anthropomorphic qualities, and also of the intellectualism that censors out supposedly extraneous information to highlight what it considers central. Traditional realists would accumulate such details as a way of indicating sensibility; neorealists posit nothing beyond the work itself and what can be derived from it.

It is the materiality of signs that characterizes abstract expressionism, innovative fiction, photorealism, and neorealism alike and constitutes their essentially spatial nature. As such, signs are most emphatically things in themselves rather than transparent windows to something else. When the sign becomes the action of paint on the canvas, the materials of this process take on added importance. Color and line are then less crucial than paint itself, de Kooning laying it on thick and heavy with one color swirling into another. Hofmann's canvases are even thicker, three-dimensional mountains and valleys of knife-applied paint; Pollock heightened the effect of his drips and splashes by mixing glass and sand into his already thickened industrial-base paint. Variations of light and color might give the sensation of depth, but these works would never rely on an illusion of spatial perspective—the space we see is the space there really is, in hard, material terms. Painting becomes an extension rather than a window or door, with the scale of that extension being the painter's body and its setting the physical limits of the canvas. What in previous undertakings had been limitations—the textural qualities of paint, the hard flatness of the canvas surface—now become the dominant features, for materiality of process is now the point.

Photorealistic paintings are hard and flat as well. Although there is a recognizable figure in such works, it is one that has been sought out precisely because the nature of its surface—the sharp reflection of glass and polished metal, the urban iconography of stark image and harsh color, and the absence of any depictable human presence—lends itself to a material rendering. The photorealists' tools enhance this flatness: quick-drying paints, often applied with an airbrush, on a canvas gelled to the point of impenetrability. The amount of concrete, steel and chrome, and glass and neon in the average photorealistic painting is as remarkable as the quantities of splashed paint and swirled line in a work of abstract expressionism, and the effect is in principle the same: a flatness which defies the illusionism of image in favor of the materials that make it up.

The neorealistic writers share a similar regard for materiality, knowing that the materials of their fictions are signs, opaque signifiers which by virtue of photorealistic treatment can become just as apparent as the painter's line and color. In such stories and novels the characters do not so much act in certain ways as they make signs of acting, a manner that Gilles Deleuze can trace back to Proust, as discussed in *Proust and Signs* (New York: Braziller, 1972, trans. Richard Howard):

> One does not think and one does not act, but one makes signs. Nothing funny is said at the Verdurins, and Mme. Verdurin does not laugh; but Cottard makes a sign that he is saying something funny, Mme. Verdurin makes a sign that she is laughing, and her sign is so perfectly emitted that M. Verdurin, not to be outdone, seeks in his turn for an appropriate mimicry. Mme. de Guermantes has a heart which is often hard, a mind which is often weak, but she always has charming signs. She does not act for her friends, she does not think with them, she makes signs to them. The worldly sign does not refer to something, it "stands for" it, claims to be equivalent to its meaning. It anticipates action as it does thought, annuls thought as it does action, and declares itself adequate: whence its stereotyped aspect, and its vacuity. (pp. 6–7)

To write this way is to paint like Richard Estes, with similar results. His paintings are not of streetcorners but of signs of streetcorners, quite often with an emphasis on the building's signs (as in advertisements) themselves. The result is a spatial outlay of materials which cannot be appreciated for what they represent, for there is no representation involved other than capturing the materiality of representation in process.

For space to function as a plane for composition, artistic action must happen on the surface. Abstract expressionists and innovative fictionists demonstrate this in every work, but in photorealism and neorealism there is the added benefit of incorporating figures which make the same point in analogical manner. Consider Walter Abish's *How German Is It* (New York: New Directions, 1980), where a German Federal

Republic Abish has never visited is portrayed exclusively in terms of elements apparent on the surface, a technique that sociologists might find appropriate to postwar German life's emphasis on materialism and certainly indicative of its great material success. Yet fiction's great advantage in this respect is its linguistic nature, for language is first of all a system operating within the surface of its own network. Abish's novella, *This Is Not a Film. This Is a Precise Act of Disbelief,* collected in *Minds Meet* (New York: New Directions, 1975), begins with the advice that "This is a familiar world" and from there charts out an action that, like language, can only develop systematically and on a thoroughly apparent surface:

> It is a world crowded with familiar faces and events. Thanks to language the brain can digest, piece by piece, what has occurred and what may yet occur. It is never at a loss for the word that signifies what is happening this instant. In Mrs. Ite's brain the interior of her large house with a view of the garden and the lake are surfaces of the familiar. She is slim, and moves quite gracefully from one familiar interior to the next. Her movements are impelled by familiar needs. (p. 31)

The novella's plot follows from this theory that human needs are shaped by the surface of what is available—in this case, by language. Just as in *Alphabetical Africa* Abish's characters cannot kiss, for example, until chapter K makes that word available, in *This Is Not a Film* the narrative can only spread over the surface that has been made available. In each case the emphasis of what would otherwise be temporal—*when* will the lovers first kiss, *how* will Mrs. Ite comprehend her husband's suicide—becomes spatial, as readers wait not for an event to happen but for a letter to appear (the alphabet's inevitability being a spatial form rather than a temporal one and based in relationship rather than sequence for everything but ordering) and not for something new to happen but to see how the present elements will combine.

In his novella Abish reinforces his linguistic system with analogical terms within his figurative story. He sets in motion the action of a French filmmaker, modeled on Godard, who has come to America so he might examine the plans and construction of an intercity shopping mall, a subject that intrigues him for its ability to structure the void of suburban life and its material impulses. Abish, trained and once employed as a city planner, sees that the three levels of activity—mall building, filmmaking, and language—are all predicated on the availability of surface (urban topography and economic life, the celluloid strip, and generative grammar), and his novella works its way through narrative just like the unfolding and refolding alphabet of his earlier work. As always, he is intrigued by the structuring role of system, as he explained in his *Fiction International* interview from fall 1975: "I was fascinated to discover the extent to which a system could impose upon the contents of a work meaning which was fashioned by the form, and then to see the degree to which the form, because of the conspicuous obstacles, undermined that very meaning" (p. 96). Thus the spatiality of this system, working as it does on the surface of its own existence, effaces any priority of form over feature or vice versa by making both dependent upon the conditions of the narrative's own activity—it is, after all, not some verifiable content or meaning-oriented subject matter that is being structured but rather a void, for which neither can claim precedence. Even the characters in Abish's novella can delight in such life upon the surface, free from authorial rage for meaning. Ping-pong is their favorite sport, and the champion at it loves to live his life the same way, operating his forklift truck at work to rearrange cases of Pepsi on an asphalt parking lot. The shopping mall creates a topology of need, the syntax within which Abish's people will cheerfully generate their sentences and plot out their lives free from anything beyond the system that makes possible their very existence.

No longer conventions in the service of something else, the signs of such narrative are removed from the purpose that would have given them transparency; we have no idea what may be around the corner from Richard Estes's drugstore or what Walter Abish's ping-pong champ will do later in the day. There is no meaning to be imposed, just a syntax of signs that will work out their activity according to the system by which they can operate and the surface over which they can spread. Above all, neither painter nor author need be troubled with representing content or subject, for the system takes care of that as a fully evident activity. With that established both author and reader are free to deal with the purely artistic problems of execution and reception. And these are on the level of sign, the spatial context in which structuralization takes place.

Index

Jerome Klinkowitz is Professor of English and a
University Distinguished Scholar at the University
of Northern Iowa. He is the author of thirty books,
including *Donald Barthelme: An Exhibition* (Duke
University Press, 1991).

Library of Congress Cataloging-in-Publication Data
Klinkowitz, Jerome.
Structuring the void : the struggle for subject in
contemporary American Fiction / Jerome
Klinkowitz.
Includes index.
ISBN 0-8223-1205-0
1. American fiction—20th century—History and
criticism.   2. Postmodernism (Literature)—United
States.   3. Literary form.   I. Title.
PK374.P64K5   1992
813'.5409—dc20   91-24113 CIP